IMAGES
of America

TOPEKA

Balloon flight became quite popular, worldwide, at the beginning of the 20th century. Above, the natural gas–filled balloon *Topeka II*, flown by Topeka pilot Frank M. Jacobs, and a second balloon prepare for liftoff. The balloons were used for both pleasure flights and racing. On June 13, 1911, Arthur J. Carruth Jr., then a writer for the *Topeka State Journal*, photographed Topeka from the air for the first time in Jacobs's balloon *Topeka I*. Photographs of that flight can be seen on pages 48 and 49. (Courtesy Don Harmon.)

ON THE COVER: A crowd gathered at the Atchison, Topeka, and Santa Fe Railroad depot in May 1903 to welcome U.S. president Theodore Roosevelt to Topeka. Roosevelt stayed overnight at the Throop Hotel, and the next day the president laid the cornerstone of the Railroad YMCA building. Roosevelt, elected as vice president to William McKinley in 1900, assumed the presidency in 1901 when McKinley was assassinated. Roosevelt won the 1904 presidential election by a large margin. (Courtesy Kansas State Historical Society.)

IMAGES
of America
TOPEKA

Greg A. Hoots

ARCADIA
PUBLISHING

Published by Arcadia Publishing
Charleston, South Carolina

Library of Congress Control Number: 2010922156

For all general information contact Arcadia Publishing at:
Telephone 843-853-2070
Fax 843-853-0044
E-mail sales@arcadiapublishing.com
For customer service and orders:
Toll-Free 1-888-313-2665

Visit us on the Internet at www.arcadiapublishing.com

*I dedicate this book to Don Harmon,
whose love for historic Topeka photographs is only exceeded
by his generosity in sharing them with others. Thanks.*

CONTENTS

ACKNOWLEDGMENTS

I would like to thank all of the organizations and individuals who have made this publication possible. In this book I have tried to display the greatest historic photographs ever taken of Topeka. Without the generosity of all of the contributors, I could have never made this unique collection available.

First, I want to acknowledge the Kansas State Historical Society for the huge contribution of photographs for this book. I could not have completed this book without the efforts of Nancy Sherbert, curator of photographs at the Kansas State Archives. Likewise, a special thanks goes to Michael Church, who manages the photographic reproductions for the state archives, as well as creating digital images for Kansasmemory.org. I would also like to thank Susan Marchant, Jeanne Mithen, and the staff at the Topeka and Shawnee County Pubic Library (TSCPL) Special Collections room for their generous contributions to this effort. Thank you to Danny San Romani, the curator of the Combat Air Museum at Forbes Field, for his help in locating and identifying photographs of Forbes Air Force Base. I would also like to thank an old friend, Don Harmon, for his generosity in providing me photographic images and for his inspiring enthusiasm. Thanks to Lloyd Zimmer, who was so generous to allow me to cherry-pick through his exceptional Topeka photograph collection. A big thanks goes to Douglass Wallace for his sharp eye and endless knowledge of Topeka history and architecture. I would also like to thank Michael Worswick for sharing his time and memories of his uncle Harold B. Wolfe. Finally, I want to extend a special thanks to Susan Wolfe for her generous contribution of photographs of her grandfather Harold B. Wolfe.

In preparing this book, I was gratified by all of the contributors' enthusiasm for the project and for their generosity in making these images available for everyone to enjoy. Every photograph contribution was important, and I thank you all.

A special note of appreciation goes to my wife, Cheryl, who is always supportive of my interest in photographic history.

INTRODUCTION

If there were one mission that this book attempts to achieve, it hopes to provide an accessible source of historic photographs of Topeka made widely available to the public at a reasonable price. Arcadia Publishing's Images of America series gives the photograph historian the ability to showcase more than 200 high-resolution images in a single volume.

In developing the material and format for this book, I sought to obtain the best photographs from the best historic photograph collections of Topeka. Although a few of these images have appeared in books and other publications, those images have been included in this collection because of their specific historic significance. The vast majority of the photographs that appear in this book have never been published before. Additionally, the dozens of Topeka history books that have been published in the last 125 years are all currently out of print. While used copies of most of these books can be found, finding a new copy of many of the titles is impossible. Images of America: *Topeka* hopes to become the handbook of Topeka historic photography.

This book is divided into six chapters, and my hope is that these photographs provide a visual link to Topeka's past. Chapter one displays 84 historical Topeka images dating from about 1860 to 1950. This chapter features the icons of Topeka architecture, the majority of which have passed from the city's landscape. Chapter two tells the story of Don Harmon, a man who became obsessed with collecting historical Topeka real-photo postcards, creating a museum-quality collection of photographic images of the town where he was born and raised. Chapter three examines the life and work of Harold B. Wolfe, the most prolific professional photographer in the history of Topeka. Wolfe began his career as a commercial photographer in Topeka in 1924, operating stores in the city until his death in 1966. The volume of photographic work that he produced in those 40 years and the extraordinary quality of his work makes his photographic portfolio the most significant in the history of the city. Chapter four takes a look at the history of the Topeka Free Fair and of the fairgrounds. This chapter includes 19 images from Topeka fairs of the past, including eight spectacular photographs from the "Free Fair Album" at the Kansas State Archives. Chapter five examines the history of Forbes Air Force Base, which was located on the south edge of Topeka for 30 years. By 1961, the facility had grown to become the most powerful air force base in the world during its assignment as a Strategic Air Command installation. Chapter six looks at five significant historic days and moments in the history of the city. Included in this group are photographic images of the 1903 flood, the Great Depression, the 1951 flood, the schools involved in the 1954 Brown vs. Board of Education decision, and the June 8, 1966, tornado. All of these events helped shape Topeka's history and its future.

More than half of the photographic images for this book were acquired from the Kansas State Archives. This collection is without comparison, containing more than 1 million photographs. In 2007, a significant event took place at the Kansas State Historical Society's State Archives. On October 16, 2007, the Web site Kansasmemory.org was launched, providing photographic images and scans of original historical documents available for viewing on the Internet. The Web site opened featuring 20,000 items, and within two years, the number of items displayed exceeded 82,000. By 2011, the sesquicentennial of Kansas statehood, the Kansas Memory Web site will display more than 100,000 images, documents, and film. The site is designed to aid classroom teachers in the presentation of historical materials to students and to be a research aid. The goal of the Kansas Memory project was to improve the public's access to historical documents and photographs located in the state's archives. The site is free to all users, and it is impressive.

The birth of the Kansas Memory project marked a new era for the Kansas State Historical Society. Prior to 2007, when a person used the research facility at the state archives and desired to have a copy of a photograph from the collection, an actual camera photograph would be taken of the original, creating a negative that would then be enlarged and printed. Unfortunately, no matter how carefully the technician focused the camera and set the lighting, there was some detail lost in the reproduction. When the Kansas Memory Web site opened, the state archives began to exclusively use digital scanning for all photographic reproductions. The improvement in the quality of the reproduced images was immediate and significant. The digital scanner could detect shadows and details of the original image that a camera's lens could never define. So there were actually two great achievements realized with the birth of the Kansas Memory Web site: public accessibility to documents and photographs in the state's collection greatly improved, reaching into classrooms and Kansans' homes across the state; and the quality of reproductions that the state could provide to researchers, writers, students, and citizens improved vastly.

Finally, to find the material and the funding available to produce a volume such as this book is a difficult task, at best. I began acquiring material for a publication of historical Topeka photographs more than 10 years ago. However, difficulties in acquiring funding and developing a distribution network for a historical photograph publication kept the project from becoming a reality until now. I am deeply indebted to the Kansas State Library and Archives for its support of this project. Therefore, I have assigned half of all of my royalties from sales of this book for the lifetime of its printing to the Kansas State Historical Society. The work that its members do to preserve Kansas' history and share it with its citizens cannot be overstated. So, every copy of Images of America: Topeka purchased helps fund the programs and facilities maintained by the Kansas State Historical Society, including the state archives that provided so many photographs for this book.

Hopefully, this publication will become a source book for anyone studying Topeka's history and its architecture. Also, I hope that my book will serve to entertain the reader, allowing him or her to view images from the past and, in some cases, reminisce with their own memories of Topeka.

One

A Photographic History of Topeka

Chapter one of this book presents photographs from the first 100 years of Topeka's history. Although the photographs are presented in a general chronological order, there are numerous exceptions. The 84 photographs presented in this chapter are not intended to tell a single story of Topeka's history, but rather, every photograph tells a story of its own.

Approximately 15 photographs dating from the Kansas territorial days through the 1870s are displayed in the beginning of this chapter. It is significant to note that in 1860, just prior to Kansas' statehood, the population of Topeka was 759. By 1870, the city's population had increased more than 600 percent to a respectable 5,790 inhabitants. The photographs from the first 15 years of the city's existence depict a town that was essentially located in the 400 and 500 block of Kansas Avenue, extending sparsely two or three blocks from that central site. A number of the business buildings that existed in Topeka prior to statehood in 1861 were wooden-frame structures. An equal number were built of native limestone, a material plentiful in the area.

A second group of photographs features buildings that were constructed during Topeka's construction boom enjoyed in the 1880s. It has been frequently reported that there were 3,000 buildings under construction in 1888. Likewise, with the new growth and available jobs, many people were moving to Topeka. The 1890 census revealed that the city had doubled in size during the previous decade, now boasting a population of 31,007. Although the construction boom experienced in Topeka in the 1880s came to an end in 1890 with an economic depression, the construction achieved during that decade set Topeka on the road to growth and prosperity in the years to come.

The third period of time featuring major changes in the architectural landscape of the city was during the first 10 years of the 20th century. Topeka experienced a new resurgence in construction, particularly during the last half of that decade. The population rebounded after the slow growth of the 1890s, and by 1910, Topeka had 43,684 residents, a growth rate of 30 percent for the decade. By 1910, the Topeka business district had stretched south to Tenth Avenue, and many of the early buildings constructed during territorial days were being demolished and replaced with new, modern structures. Most of the early business buildings suffered from the absence of central heat, modern plumbing, and electrical wiring, and many were replaced for those reasons. Frequently, however, the early structures were replaced when fire damaged or destroyed them.

Topeka experienced its next era of growth and prosperity in the 1920s. A number of new buildings were constructed in downtown, and the city's population increased to more than 60,000. It was during this decade that the city's first skyscrapers were built, including the National Reserve Life building at the southeast corner of Tenth and Kansas Avenues, the new Capitol Savings and Loan building at 534 Kansas Avenue, and two new hotels, the Jayhawk Hotel at Seventh and Jackson Streets and the Kansan Hotel at Ninth Street and Kansas Avenue.

The decade of the 1930s was one of difficulty for Topeka residents, not unlike the despair that all of America felt during the Great Depression. The failure of businesses and lending institutions led to a spiral of economic collapse that was only assuaged by the creation of various state and federal public works relief projects and programs. A majority of the construction projects initiated during the 1930s were funded by government subsidies. One notable exception was the private construction of the ultra-modern National Bank of Topeka building at 535 Kansas Avenue, completed in 1932. Virtually all of the federal- or state-funded public works projects were carefully photographed upon completion, and many of them were photographed during construction. The budgets for every government project included money for photographing and documenting the results, thus creating an excellent photographic history of the era.

The 1940s was a decade of little growth in Topeka. With the declaration of war in December 1941, Topeka experienced rationing of gasoline and other commodities, and construction of any non-war-related buildings dwindled. One bright spot in Topeka's future was the opening of the Topeka Army Airfield in August 1942. The precursor to Forbes Air Force Base, the airfield brought millions of dollars in defense department money into the Topeka economy. The air base would be a vital part of Topeka's economy for 30 years, prior to its closing in 1973. Forbes Air Force Base was a major factor in stimulating the Topeka economy in the 1950s when the Strategic Air Command moved into the facility in 1951. A second milestone in the 1940s was the construction of the Goodyear tire plant in North Topeka in 1944. Goodyear constructed the plant for the U.S. government but then purchased the facility in 1945 for production of civilian tires. Goodyear would be a major employer in Topeka for decades to come.

By 1960, Topeka had reached a milestone; it was the first census in which the city's population exceeded 100,000. Topeka began to expand in every direction, especially to the west. After the Topeka population reached the plateau of 119,484 in 1960, it would become impossible to maintain the double-digit growth figures that the city experienced during many of the decades in its past. Topeka's geographical limitations had established the saturation point with respect to population. The rural areas of Shawnee County began to see significant growth during the last quarter of the 20th century, as individuals and families who worked in Topeka chose to live in a suburban or even rural atmosphere.

There are two factors that historically allowed Topeka to sustain growth despite periods of economic downturn. The first, and most important, factor is that since statehood in 1861, Topeka has been both the state capital and the county seat. Government jobs have maintained stability in the local economy, giving Topeka an advantage enjoyed by no other city in Kansas. The second factor contributing to the stability of Topeka's economy has been the city's ability to attract and keep major employers in the private sector. For example, for more than a century Topeka has been the home of the Atchison, Topeka, and Santa Fe Railroad, now known as the Burlington Northern Santa Fe Railroad, a major employer in the capital city. Throughout the 20th century, Topeka has been able to attract a wide array of manufacturing and distributing businesses that have sustained growth in its economy.

At almost every step, the growth and development of Topeka can be seen in photographs of the time. The images in this chapter provide almost a time-lapse view of the expansion of the city from its roots, when the business district was just two blocks in length.

This map, created in 1855, was the original plan for streets and public buildings in Topeka. The hand-drawn map is attributed to one of the founders of Topeka, Franklin Crane, who created the document for the Topeka Association. It denotes the width of the streets, avenues, and alleys and provides a detailed numbering of each lot in every block. (Courtesy Kansas State Historical Society.)

This view of the west side of Kansas Avenue during Topeka's territorial days looks south from Sixth Avenue. These were among the first business buildings constructed at Topeka's original town site. F. W. Giles's bank building (at right) and Topeka Drug Store (607 Kansas Avenue, center) were two early territorial businesses in Topeka. This photograph was taken by W. H. Bliss, Photographic Car, a noted territorial-days photographer. (Courtesy Kansas State Historical Society.)

This W. P. Bliss, Photographic Car view of the east side of the 600 block of Kansas Avenue shows the abundance of wooden-frame buildings in downtown Topeka during the territorial period. Businesses shown in this c. 1860 view include the Topeka Meat Market; J. F. Osenburg, Saddle and Harness Manufacturer; Capitol Meat Market; and the Provision Feed-Seed Store. (Courtesy Kansas State Historical Society.)

This Paul Boeger photograph, taken around 1870, shows considerable signs of construction on Kansas Avenue after statehood. Notice the Topeka Drug Store (opposite) can be seen at right in this view. The first wing of the state capitol building can be seen on the horizon to the right. The stone building with three chimneys in the center of the photograph is the Tefft House hotel (635 Kansas Avenue), built in 1859. (Courtesy Kansas State Historical Society.)

This mid-1870s view looks south from Sixth Avenue at the west side of Kansas Avenue showing buildings occupying almost every lot. Businesses seen (from right to left) include Kansas Valley National Bank, Orrin T. Welch Land Office, Topeka Drug Store, City Bakery, S. Barnum and Company Dry Goods, Express Wagon Delivery, and an unidentified drug store. Again, the Tefft House can be identified at far left by its chimneys. (Courtesy Kansas State Historical Society.)

13

A team of six oxen pulling Theodore Krippe's wagon has stopped at the northwest corner of Sixth and Kansas Avenues in this snowy view, taken around 1870. The men seen near the wagon are unidentified, but the buildings are, from left to right, the Gleed Building, 535 Kansas Avenue; C. Bowman, Merchant Tailor; and Horne's Land Office and Insurance Agency. This intersection was the center of the early Topeka business district. (Courtesy Kansas State Historical Society.)

This 1871 view of Kansas Avenue looking north from Sixth Avenue shows the construction of a fire cistern, located in the center of the intersection. Used from 1870 to 1882, water was drawn from the Kansas River and pumped into the cisterns by the fire department. Above, a team of mules pulls a wagon filled with excavated dirt. Notice bricks and sand in the street, as new buildings were being constructed. (Courtesy Kansas State Historical Society.)

Wagons lined the street as settlers stopped for supplies in Topeka before journeying to the frontier. This *c.* 1880 photograph looks to the south from Sixth Avenue at the east side of the 500 block of Kansas Avenue. Today this is the site of Townsite One Plaza bank tower. The same block can be seen 30 years later in an image on the bottom of page 57. (Courtesy Kansas State Historical Society.)

In 1868, George W. Crane and J. Y. Byron formed the Crane and Bryon printing business in the Ritchie block. They lost everything in a November 1869 fire before moving to this building, located at 713–715 Kansas Avenue. In addition to bookbinding and commercial printing, the firm printed the *Commonwealth* daily newspaper, which was popular in the 1870s. The business was lost again when this building burned in October 1873. (Courtesy Kansas State Historical Society.)

Located at the southwest corner of Fifth and Quincy Streets, the Fifth Avenue Hotel was among the finest establishments in the city. When construction began in 1870, the building was intended to be an implement warehouse, but construction was altered in 1871, and the building was completed as a hotel. The building was said to have 21 chimneys; every guest room was equipped with a stove, as the hotel had no central heat. In 1872, Grand Duke Alexis, son of Russian tsar Alexander II, visited Topeka, staying at the Fifth Avenue Hotel while on a buffalo hunt in western Kansas. Accompanying the duke were Buffalo Bill Cody, Gen. Phil Sheridan, and Brig. Gen. George Custer. The hotel went through a number of owners before closing on April 22, 1958, and being razed on December 7, 1960. (Courtesy Lloyd Zimmer.)

This W. P. Bliss photograph from the early 1860s shows three businesses located on the west side of the 400 block of Kansas Avenue. Immediately to the south of these buildings was Constitution Hall. Seen are, from left to right, the Merchants Union Express Company; the Topeka Post Office, and Holmburg and Morris. In Kansas territorial days, most of the merchants used lot numbers to identify their business rather than modern street numbers. (Courtesy Kansas State Historical Society.)

This view, looking north from the intersection of Eighth and Kansas Avenues, was taken around 1870. The streets were mud, and no streetcar tracks had yet been laid. Notice that the wagon wheel tracks form a circle in the center of the intersection. At that time, the business district ended at Eighth Street, so horse-drawn vehicles simply turned around in the intersection. (Courtesy Kansas State Historical Society.)

Above, the west wing of the state capitol building was under construction when this 1879 photograph was taken by Cone Photography. The east wing was the first constructed; work began on that wing on October 17, 1866. The legislature began using the east wing in 1870. Below, stonemasons prepare the columns during construction of the south wing of the state capitol. Chunks of limestone were carved in sections and stacked to form columns. Each wing was built separately, with construction of the final center section beginning in 1885. Work on the dome began in 1889. Construction of the statehouse took 37 years at a cost of $3,200,588.92. (Both, courtesy Kansas State Historical Society.)

Above, the east and west wings of the state capitol building can be seen completed. To the right center of the photograph is the Topeka Free Library, originally located on the capitol grounds and constructed in 1883. In the foreground is the *Commonwealth* newspaper printing business. Below, with the four wings complete, construction of the center section of the building was finished by 1889, leaving only the copper dome and roof remaining to be done. An electric streetcar is seen going north on Jackson Street at Tenth Avenue. The state capitol is located on 20 acres donated to the state by Topeka pioneer Cyrus K. Holliday. (Both, courtesy Kansas State Historical Society.)

Fry W. Giles, one of the original founding fathers of Topeka, built this house, located at 113 West Eighth Avenue, in 1859. He lived there with his wife, Caroline, until his death in 1898. After his death, Giles's house, the oldest home in Topeka, was sold to George Burghart, who converted it into a cigar factory. In 1919, Capper Publishing purchased the house and razed it to expand the Capper building. (Courtesy Kansas State Historical Society.)

City hall was located in the Security Building, at the southwest corner of Seventh Street and Kansas Avenue, when this 1878 photograph was taken. At that time, a dry-goods store and I. N. Kneeland and Company City Drug Store occupied the first floor. To the west, on Seventh Street between Kansas Avenue and Jackson Street, one can see the new Topeka Fire Station No. 2 Headquarters (see page 31). (Courtesy Lloyd Zimmer.)

Duvall and VanHorn, Merchant Tailors, and Searle and Brother Illinois Stove Store occupied the first floor of the Gale block in this W. P. Bliss, Photographic Car view, taken around 1864. Located on the east side of the 600 block of Kansas Avenue, the Gale block was an early territorial building used by the Kansas Legislature for meetings in the 1860s. (Courtesy Kansas State Historical Society.)

Rodgers Brothers Grocers was located on lot No. 132 on the east side of the 400 block of Kansas Avenue, generally speaking, across the street from the Merchants Union Express building seen at the top of page 17. This c. 1870 photograph shows the Rodgers building, an early Kansas Avenue frame building constructed shortly after statehood, with two delivery wagons unloading merchandise. (Courtesy Kansas State Historical Society.)

Workers seen here are laying paving bricks in the 400 block of Kansas Avenue. The four businesses identified in the center of this photograph include, from left to right, F. P. Zimmerman Meat Market (408), Nick Schaefer Bakery (414), Wolf and Powell boots and shoes (416), and Capitol Insurance Company, F. W. Hatch Agency (418). Notice the horse-drawn streetcar moving north on the avenue. (Courtesy Kansas State Historical Society.)

As the city converted from horse-drawn streetcars to electric-powered ones in 1896, lines expanded, and the need to lay new track grew. In this view looking north, workers lay track at the intersection of Sixth and Kansas Avenues. Notice that the Gleed building, located at the northwest corner of the intersection, had been replaced with the Mulvane Bank building, dating this view to after 1907. (Courtesy Kansas State Historical Society.)

Above, Topeka photographer W. F. Farrow captured this image of workers constructing the new *State Journal* newspaper building at the southeast corner of Eighth and Kansas Avenues. Dated June 9, 1896, workers can be seen mixing mortar for the bricklayers. In the background, the old *Daily Capital* building, the city's competing newspaper, can be seen. Below, a crowd has gathered outside the newspaper building, waiting for breaking news or perhaps the ball scores. It was common practice for the newspaper to post election results, ball scores, and breaking news from the wire service in the front window of the building. This Farrow photograph is dated 1904. (Both, courtesy Lloyd Zimmer.)

This W. F. Farrow photograph, dated 1891, looks to the north from the intersection of Sixth and Kansas Avenues. At the far left one can see the Gleed Building, housing the Bank of Topeka, at 535 Kansas Avenue; and at the right edge of the photograph is the first Capitol Building and Loan Association building, at 534 Kansas Avenue. The tower to the right of center is the old federal building. (Courtesy Lloyd Zimmer.)

This 1896 photograph shows the construction of the Melan bridge (center), which crossed the river at Kansas Avenue. At left is the railroad bridge, and to the right is the old iron bridge, constructed privately in 1870 and sold to the city in 1871. The Melan bridge suffered a collapse of several sections of floor on July 2, 1965, killing one motorist whose car fell into the river. (Courtesy Kansas State Historical Society.)

24

The five Rehkopf brothers operated a carriage works at 207–209 West Sixth Avenue, first constructing horse-drawn carriages and then, with the advent of the automobile, began creating bodies for commercial trucks. Above, this Rehkopf Brothers truck was built for the *Topeka Daily Capital* newspaper. Other Rehkopf trucks can be seen on page 37. (Courtesy Kansas State Historical Society.)

Newspaper delivery boys pose in front of the first Daily Capital building, also known as the Hudson building, named for the newspaper's first owner, Maj. J. K. Hudson. The building was located at the southeast corner of Eighth Avenue and Quincy Street. Originally a morning paper, in 1881 the *Capital* became an afternoon edition. In 1901, Arthur Capper's family purchased the paper, and he became its sole owner in 1904. (Courtesy Kansas State Historical Society.)

The Thacher building was constructed in 1888, a year when 3,000 buildings were under construction in Topeka. Located at 110 East Eighth Avenue, the building was designed by architect John G. Haskell, and its first tenant was Hall and O'Donald printers. In 1899, Crane and Company printers moved into the building, where it remained for a century. This photograph dates from 1890; a later view can be seen on page 74. (Courtesy Kansas State Historical Society.)

A horse-drawn steam-powered fire engine heads north to a fire in the 600 block of Quincy Street. Ezra Robinson (left) and William J. Cawker are manning the wagon in this 1908 view. Stonestreet and Hamilton Undertakers can be seen above at 636 Quincy Street. On January 5, 1870, the city held a referendum to purchase the first fire engine. Interestingly, no one voted. In February, the city purchased the engine. (Courtesy Kansas State Historical Society.)

Members of the Topeka Police Department pose in front of the Crawford Building, located at the southwest corner of Fifth and Jackson Streets. The police station was located across Fifth Street to the north. This view, by photographer J. C. Irvin, was taken around 1900. The old police station was replaced in 1937 with a new headquarters on the same site. The new police station can be seen on page 82. (Courtesy Kansas State Historical Society.)

The city railway station horsecar barn was located on the north side of Tenth Avenue, between Kansas Avenue and Jackson Street. This c. 1885 view shows railway workers posing at the south side of the building. To the left one can see the Kansas capitol building in the background. Horse-drawn trolley service ended in May 1896, and electric streetcar service ended in Topeka on July 18, 1937. (Courtesy Kansas State Historical Society.)

The Topeka Railway Transfer Station was located at the southwest corner of Eighth and Kansas Avenues when this photograph was taken on November 8, 1893. The two uniformed men standing in the center of the photograph are Charles Hixon (left) and Frank Stitt. The streetcar railway service began on June 1, 1881, and by 1885, Topeka boasted more than 8 miles of track, 25 coaches, 32 employees, and 95 animals. (Courtesy Kansas State Historical Society.)

Construction on the Young Men's Christian Association (YMCA) was nearing completion when this *c.* 1907 photograph was taken. The YMCA was located at the northwest corner of Ninth and Quincy Streets. Just to the west, at 110 East Ninth Street, is the small shop of building contractor J. L. Eddy. At the far left is the state capitol, and to its right one can see the dome of the First Baptist Church. (Courtesy Special Collections, TSCPL.)

A Topeka Rapid Transit Railway streetcar is stopped in front of Joseph Bromich's Topeka Steam Boiler Works business, located at 117–119 Jefferson Street. This view dates to the late 1880s. This was one of the many buildings and homes that were demolished with the coming of urban renewal in the late 1960s. Topeka Rapid Transit Railway, incorporated in 1887, was purchased by Topeka Railway Company in 1892. (Courtesy Special Collections, TSCPL.)

Above, the Veale-Thompson block, designed by J. G. Haskell and located at 621–627 Southwest Quincy Street, was built during the 1887–1888 construction boom in Topeka. Here, stonemasons are facing the ornate building with cut limestone. Below, the Veale-Thompson block can be seen here completed with businesses occupying the bottom floor while the upstairs contained apartment dwellings. The building was refaced in 1945 in an attempt to modernize its appearance; however, it continued to fall into disrepair, and in 1951, the building was demolished. The property was converted to parking. The finest ornamental stonework in the history of the city was created in the last half of the 19th century. (Above, courtesy Kansas State Historical Society; below, courtesy Special Collections, TSCPL.)

Above, Fire Station No. 2, built in 1878, was located on the south side of Seventh Street, between Kansas Avenue and Jackson Street. For many years this was the department headquarters. Another view of this station appears on page 20. At left is a chemical wagon, a fire extinguisher apparatus, while a hose wagon and Chief George O. Wilmarth's buggy are displayed at right. Below, Fire Station No. 3, constructed at 312 Jefferson Street in 1882, was manned exclusively with African Americans from its opening until 1963. In 1886, a second story was added to the structure, and in 1929, the building received a new front and overhead door. Although there was some controversy when integration of the department was discussed by the city council, the process went smoothly when implemented. (Both, courtesy Special Collections, TSCPL.)

A crowd gathered at the Atchison, Topeka, and Santa Fe Railroad (ATSF) depot in May 1903 to welcome U.S. president Theodore Roosevelt to Topeka. Roosevelt visited Topeka to lay the cornerstone of the Railroad YMCA building, located at 706–712 East Fourth Street. While in Topeka, Roosevelt spent the night at the Throop Hotel. The brick ATSF depot, located at Fifth and Holiday Streets, opened in 1881 and was used until 1949. (Courtesy Kansas State Historical Society.)

Built in 1869, the first Atchison, Topeka, and Santa Fe Railroad depot in Topeka was located on the west side of the mainline, at the southwest corner of Fourth and Washington Streets. This J. R. Riddle photograph is dated 1880. Notice the number of chimneys protruding from the roof. The building had no boiler heat. Instead, it relied on coal stoves in all of the rooms in the depot. (Courtesy Kansas State Historical Society.)

The National Reserve Life Insurance Company building, located at the southeast corner of Tenth and Kansas Avenues, was bedecked for a gala event on August 18, 1928, Notification Day for Topeka's native son, vice president candidate and U.S. senator Charles Curtis. It was the custom for the presidential and vice presidential candidates to speak in their hometown, notifying their constituents of their candidacy for office. This International Newsreel photograph describes the event as "the biggest day in the history of the city." Curtis and presidential candidate Herbert Hoover won the election over Democrat Al Smith, making Curtis the first vice president from Kansas, as well as the first born west of the Mississippi River. Other views of the National Reserve building can be seen on pages 84 and 127. (Courtesy Greg Hoots.)

The north side of the 100 block of West Sixth Avenue is seen in this 1902 photograph. Buildings seen from left to right include the Topeka Hotel, the Palace Hotel, unidentified, the Columbian building, unidentified, the south side of the Gleed Building, and on the northeast corner of Sixth and Kansas Avenues, Capitol Building and Loan Association. Only the Columbian building survives today. (Courtesy Lloyd Zimmer.)

The city hall and auditorium (above) were constructed at the southeast corner of Seventh and Quincy Streets in 1900 at a total cost of $95,811. A fire station was located at the far end of the building, as seen above in this c. 1910 photograph. This building was demolished to make way for the new $1.5 million municipal auditorium, constructed with a Public Works Administration grant in 1939. (Courtesy Special Collections, TSCPL.)

This photograph of the Crosby Brothers Company department store, located at 717–719 Kansas Avenue, dates to the early 1900s. Crosby Brothers opened for business in 1880, and the business was moved to this location in 1895. When the business closed in 1975, it was the oldest department store in the history of Topeka. Notice the carriage and mail wagon parked in front of the building. (Courtesy Kansas State Historical Society.)

When S. S. Kresge constructed this new store at 619 Kansas Avenue in the early 1910s, it was one of several Kresge stores in Topeka. In this photograph, Union Dentists, Roberts Furs and Dr. J. N. Beasley all maintained offices on the second floor. This building replaced the Western Union building and Crockett's Clothing building, located at 619–621 Kansas Avenue, seen on page 59. (Courtesy Kansas State Historical Society.)

Above, Topeka firemen fought this blaze at the Palace Clothiers, located at 709–711 Kansas Avenue, in this 1916 photograph. Below, the Parkhurst Davis Mercantile Company building, located at the northwest corner of First and Kansas Avenues, is seen here after firefighters fought throughout the night of February 13, 1904, battling this blaze. Topeka suffered three major fires in the downtown area and numerous house fires before the Topeka Fire Department was created in 1870. In July 1882, the city created the water department, laying 15 miles of mains and installing 150 double hydrants. Prior to that time, the fire department had to rely on cisterns buried on Kansas Avenue or had to haul water to the fire. (Both, courtesy Kansas State Historical Society.)

Above, this new lumber delivery truck for J. Thomas Lumber Company, located at 213 West Sixth Avenue, was bodied by Rehkopf Brothers carriage builders, located next door at 207–209 West Sixth Avenue. Below, this moving van was manufactured by Rehkopf Brothers for the Topeka Transfer and Storage Company, whose warehouse was located at 528 Adams Street. Topeka Transfer and Storage Company is a longtime Topeka business, founded in 1880, and it is still in operation today. (Both, courtesy Kansas State Historical Society.)

PHOTO BY BOEGER

Above, the interior of the A. K. Longren Aircraft Works plant, located at 420 Jackson Street, can be seen in this Paul Boeger photograph, taken around 1916. Entire aircraft were built by hand in this facility. Below, Albin K. Longren's first flight in airplane No. 1 is seen here on September 2, 1911. The airplane's engine was an 8-cylinder, water-cooled Type A-2 Hall-Scott, producing 60 horsepower. Amazingly, Longren had no experience or training as a pilot; however, he was the first man to construct an aircraft in Kansas that was successfully flown. He successfully completed 1,372 exhibition flights in his aircraft. (Both, courtesy Kansas State Historical Society.)

Above, the Kansas State Historical Society was created by the legislature in 1875 and made its first home in the Kansas state capitol building. In 1914, the historical society and museum moved to the Memorial Building, located at Tenth Avenue and Jackson Street. In 1984, the historical society, Kansas Museum of History, and the Kansas State Archives were moved to a new complex at 6425 Southwest Sixth Avenue. (Courtesy Kansas State Historical Society.)

A large crowd gathered to watch the parade and dedication of the new Grand Army of the Republic (GAR) Memorial Hall, at the northeast corner of Tenth Avenue and Jackson Street in Topeka. U.S. president William Howard Taft laid the cornerstone for the building in 1911, and it was completed shortly before its May 30, 1914, dedication. The building was financed with federal money paid for debts to Kansas incurred during the Civil War. (Courtesy Kansas State Historical Society.)

In 1908, the Topeka Commercial Club donated land to the Sisters of Charity, Leavenworth, Kansas, on which to build a hospital. The Sisters of Charity raised money to construct the facility, and on October 17, 1909, St. Francis Hospital opened a 40-bed hospital. St. Francis Hospital and St. Francis Chapel are seen in this 1940s photograph. The hospital is still located in Topeka today at 1700 Southwest Seventh Street. (Courtesy Kansas State Historical Society.)

Christ Hospital (above) opened on May 14, 1884, in a 30-bed facility on a 20-acre tract of land on the site of the present-day Stormont-Vail Regional Health Center. In 1949, Christ Hospital, or Vail Hospital as it was known by that time, merged with the Jane C. Stormont Hospital and Training School for Nurses, founded in Topeka in 1894. This view of Christ Hospital was taken in 1908. (Courtesy Special Collections, TSCPL.)

Created by the state legislature, the Topeka Insane Asylum opened for patients on June 1, 1879, with facilities for 135 patients. In 1900, H. M. Hadley designed the administration building, seen in the center of the above photograph. In 1910, the legislature renamed the facility the Topeka State Hospital. The Topeka State Hospital closed in 1997. Interestingly, a cemetery containing 1,157 patients' graves, all but 16 unmarked, remains on the grounds. (Courtesy Kansas State Historical Society.)

In 1896, the Atchison, Topeka, and Santa Fe Railroad opened the Santa Fe Hospital for the benefit of its employees, locating it at 600 Madison Street. On February 1, 1972, the hospital changed its name to Memorial Hospital and began allowing admission of patients who were not railroad employees. In 1989, Memorial Hospital closed, and the building has been converted into retirement housing. (Courtesy Special Collections, TSCPL.)

Above, the 1907 Topeka White Socks of the Western League played ball at the Topeka Baseball Park, located at Fifteenth and Adams Streets. Local baseball was popular at the beginning of the 20th century. To accommodate fans, a streetcar rail line ran to the ballpark. From 1939 through 1954, the Topeka Owls played in the Western Association League at their ballpark, located at North Topeka Boulevard and Lyman Road. (Courtesy Lloyd Zimmer.)

Three Curtiss JN-4 aircraft are parked on this Topeka ball field in this early-1920s photograph. Curtiss manufactured these aircraft for the military as trainers during World War I. After the war, they became popular with barnstormers and daredevils. The bodies of the aircraft were wooden, making them heavy and slow in the air. The "Jenny," as the aircraft was known, had a top speed of 75 miles per hour. (Courtesy Lloyd Zimmer.)

This 1923 Wolcott photograph shows the construction of the Kansan Hotel (see page 76), located at the northeast corner of Ninth Street and Kansas Avenue. The hotel, boasting 300 rooms, opened on July 21, 1924, and was Topeka's first million-dollar hotel. After it was rebuilt from an August 6, 1948, fire, the hotel operated until 1968, when it underwent a complete renovation, converting the building into 88 apartments. (Courtesy Lloyd Zimmer.)

This aerial photograph taken from a U.S. Air Force aircraft during the 1940s shows downtown from a viewpoint over the capitol building. At the lower right is the First Baptist Church (see page 64); at right center is the Hotel Kansan; to the left of the Hotel Kansan one can see the 800 block of Kansas Avenue; and to the upper left, the new Topeka Municipal Auditorium is visible. (Courtesy Combat Air Museum.)

The First Congregational Church of Topeka was organized in 1855. Members began constructing this church in 1857, but shortly before completion in 1859, it was leveled by a tornado and then as work resumed, leveled again by winds in 1860. The church was finally completed in 1861, as seen in this W. P. Bliss photograph, and stood at the northwest corner of Seventh and Harrison Streets. (Courtesy Kansas State Historical Society.)

In the 1870s, many former slaves, known as Exodusters, settled in central Topeka in an area known as Tennessee Town. In 1893, Dr. Charles Sheldon, pastor of the Central Congregational Church, organized a kindergarten for African American children in Tennessee Town. Above, the first kindergarten class poses in front of the Union Hall Reading Room and Kindergarten, located on the east side of Lincoln Street between Munson and Twelfth Streets. (Courtesy Kansas State Historical Society.)

Established in 1865 by the Topeka Congregational Church as Lincoln College, it was renamed Washburn College in 1868, honoring Ichabod Washburn, a wealthy benefactor of the school. In 1871, the campus relocated to a 160-acre tract donated by abolitionist John Ritchie. Above, this early view of Washburn shows evidence of ongoing construction projects and dates to the late 1890s. Horse-drawn trolley service to the college began in 1888. (Courtesy Kansas State Historical Society.)

On January 29, 1861, the day of Kansas statehood, the territorial legislature, in its last act, approved the incorporation of the Episcopal Female Seminary of Topeka, located on 20 acres given to the church by the Topeka Association. Above, Wolfe Hall was completed in 1871 before the institution changed its name to College of the Sisters of Bethany in 1872. The college was located at Ninth and Polk Streets. (Courtesy Lloyd Zimmer.)

Above, workers filled the racing balloon *Topeka* with natural gas at Topeka's Westlawn Park for the June 13, 1911, flight in which the first aerial photographs of the city were taken. George S. Badders of the Topeka Commercial Club, seen here with bow tie, and Arthur Carruth Jr., at right in white hat, accompanied pilot Frank M. Jacobs on the flight. Shown at left, the balloon reached an altitude of 4,000 feet during the flight. The balloon used bags of sand for ballast, and tiny handfuls would be released to gain altitude. Likewise, a small amount of gas would be released to descend. The balloon was inflated with natural gas; thus, the filling and operation of the craft was inherently dangerous, as the gas was extremely flammable. (Both, courtesy Lloyd Zimmer.)

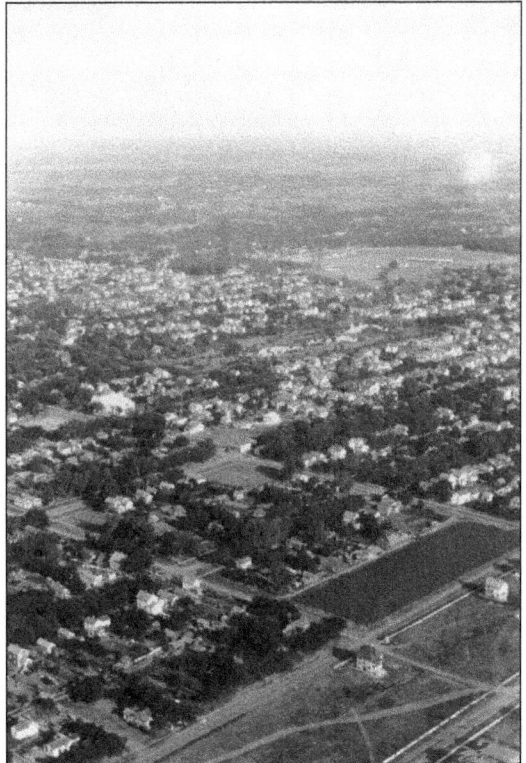

Above, Topeka balloon racer Frank Jacobs piloted the *Topeka II* in the National Balloon Race held in Kansas City on July 10, 1911. In that race he traveled 190 miles, landing in LaHarpe, Illinois. Shown at right, Arthur Carruth Jr., of the *Topeka State Journal*, took the first aerial photographs of Topeka on June 13, 1911, including this view, during his flight in the balloon named *Topeka*. As a point of reference, the racetrack at the Topeka State Fairgrounds can be seen at the upper right of the image. The flight departed Westlawn Park (the site of the Topeka Shawnee County Public Library) and landed about 6 miles southwest of Topeka. (Above, courtesy Special Collections, TSCPL; right, courtesy Lloyd Zimmer.)

Shawnee County's first courthouse in Topeka, completed in 1868, was located at 401 Kansas Avenue. To the south of the courthouse is Dutton House, an early Topeka hotel. This photograph dates from about 1880. After the new courthouse (below) was constructed, the old courthouse was refaced and converted to a hotel. Known as the Glenwood, then the Reid, and finally the Norva Hotel, it was demolished on October 9, 1977. (Courtesy Kansas State Historical Society.)

In 1884, county commissioners purchased land at the northwest corner of Fifth and Van Buren Streets for the construction of the new Shawnee County Courthouse, seen above. Considerable controversy surrounded the purchase of the land and the construction of the courthouse, as it was done without a public referendum. The courthouse and county jail were housed in this building from 1885 until the current courthouse was built in 1965. (Courtesy Greg Hoots.)

Above, Topeka's old high school was located at the northwest corner of Eighth Avenue and Harrison Street, where it opened on November 16, 1894. After the new high school was completed in September 1931, the old school became a government office building before burning on May 18, 1935. The new high school, shown at right, was known for being the first high school west of the Mississippi River to be constructed at a cost of $1 million. It is still the home of Topeka High School, located at 800 West Tenth Avenue. (Above, courtesy Special Collections, TSCPL; right, courtesy Kansas State Historical Society.)

This Registration Day parade, held June 5, 1917, honored the beginning of conscription, or the first military draft, necessitated by the United States' entry into World War I. On that day, 10 million American men registered for the draft in the first round. In this photograph, a group of Native American men is seen in the parade in the 800 block of Kansas Avenue. (Courtesy Kansas State Historical Society.)

This 1919 parade passed under the victory arch constructed across Kansas Avenue at Eighth Avenue and a banner proclaiming "Welcome Home Victorious Sons," as the 35th Infantry division returned to Kansas. The division contained members of Missouri and Kansas National Guards returning to Camp Funston for demobilization. This view looks north from Eighth Avenue. (Courtesy Kansas State Historical Society.)

In this 1930s view of the Apex Theater a group of African American schoolchildren are treated to a movie and ice cream. The Apex was located at 122 East Fourth Street and was demolished during urban renewal in the late 1960s. The Apex was listed in the "colored businesses" section of the *1930 Polk Directory*. Located at the theater was the Silver Moon Grill, an African American eatery. (Courtesy Kansas State Historical Society.)

This view of the Mosby-Mack Ford dealership, located at the northwest corner of Eleventh Street and Kansas Avenue, is dated 1935. The dealership was owned by Herbert Mack and James Mosby, until the latter's death in 1936. During its heyday, the dealership had 7 locations and 125 employees. In 1960, the Mosby-Mack Ford dealership was sold to Noller Motors. Mack continued in other business enterprises until his death in 1962. (Courtesy Kansas State Historical Society.)

Above, this 1939 view of the Gage Park swimming pool by Topeka photographer Harold B. Wolfe shows one of several improvements to the park financed by the Public Works Administration. Below, this 1925 photograph recalls a long forgotten feature of Gage Park—public camping. Written on the reverse is, "drying out our camp at Gage Park after a rain." The park, located on 160 acres at Sixth Avenue and Gage Boulevard, was gifted to the City of Topeka in 1899 by the heirs of Gilford Gage. The park is the home of the Topeka Zoo and the Helen Hocker Theater. (Above, courtesy Special Collections, TSCPL; below, courtesy Greg Hoots.)

Skelly Station No. 2, seen in this 1930s photograph, was located at the southeast corner of Sixth Avenue and Gage Boulevard. The station was built to resemble an airplane and sold Skelly Aromax–brand gasoline. The station, a notorious example of novel architecture, was a landmark in southwest Topeka from the 1920s to the 1950s. It was located diagonally across the intersection from the Old Mill Dance Hall. (Courtesy Kansas State Historical Society.)

The Old Mill Dance Hall, seen in this 1930s photograph, was located at the northwest corner of Sixth Avenue and Gage Boulevard. The entrance, built to resemble a Dutch windmill, allowed cars to pass through the base to enter the business. The Old Mill claimed to have the largest dance hall and the largest swimming pool in Kansas. Tourist cabins were also available for rental. (Courtesy Kansas State Historical Society.)

An unidentified man stands beside a large scrap metal recycling collection site, located at the southwest corner of Eighth Avenue and Jackson Street during World War II. Metal recycling, rationing of gasoline and other commodities, and a scarcity of copper and construction materials were all common occurrences during the war. These buildings, housing the Chocolate Shop Annex and Cappers Publication Annex, at 122 and 118 West Eighth Avenue, still stand today. (Courtesy Greg Hoots.)

Shawnee Motors, a Topeka Plymouth and DeSoto automobile dealer, is seen in this late-1940s night view. Located at 614 Quincy Street, the automobile dealership was owned by W. M. Vance. This building was originally constructed for George Badders's Ford dealership and was demolished to make room for the new Shawnee County Courthouse in 1965. (Courtesy Kansas State Historical Society.)

Two

DON HARMON'S TOPEKA

More than a dozen years ago, while researching historic Topeka photographs for what would ultimately become this book, a friend recommended Don Harmon, as he was known to have the largest and finest collection of Topeka real-photo postcards in existence. Harmon's collection of real-photo postcards was unmatched by any museum or other private collection in the state. Every Topeka real-photo postcard view that was ever produced, Harmon had.

Real-photo postcards have their origin in the invention of the Number 3A Folding Pocket Kodak camera in 1903. It allowed the photographer to use size 122 roll film and produce negatives that were the size of a postcard, measuring 3¼ inches by 5½ inches. The film would then be exposed by contact to a postcard blank, covered in film emulsion on one side, producing a sharp image without needing an enlarger. Most commercial photographers purchased one of these cameras, and many individuals and storeowners had one.

In 1907, U.S. postal regulations changed to began permitting a message to be written on the same side as the address of a postcard, which allowed a photograph or other image to be displayed on the reverse. With the change in that regulation, the postcard craze swept the country. Postcard collecting became popular, and merchants offered cards for sale that depicted scenes from the local area.

Don Harmon was born on February 23, 1930, at his parents' home at 900 Poplar Street in the Oakland community of Topeka. Harmon went to work for the Atchison, Topeka, and Santa Fe Railroad in 1947 in the freight traffic department in Topeka. That began a career lasting more than 40 years. Harmon married his wife, Joyce, in 1954, and when offered a promotion to chief clerk in the sales office in Oklahoma City in 1961, Harmon took the job, and they moved. Late in 1962, Harmon took a position in Denver as freight and passenger agent, where he remained until 1968. That year Harmon transferred to Wichita, where he spent six years before taking a district sales job in Chanute in 1974. In 1978, Harmon returned to Topeka, becoming the district sales manager in 1981. In 1984, Harmon moved to the Kansas City area, building a home in Shawnee, where he retired at the end of 1987. The railroad had provided a good living for Don, Joyce, and their three children. It had also provided Don an opportunity to pursue his other love, postcards.

Though Harmon moved across the country and across Kansas when employed by the ATSF, he always considered Topeka to be his home. He had begun collecting postcards casually as a child living in Topeka. In 1970, while living and working in Wichita, Harmon began collecting Topeka and ATSF railroad real-photo postcards in earnest. The hobby became an obsession. As a Santa Fe employee, Harmon had many opportunities to obtain railroad postcards, particularly those featuring depots, freight yards, and other railroad facilities. The Topeka cards were more difficult to find, especially after Harmon had obtained most of the more common views. Harmon scoured antique stores, flea markets, and auctions looking for Topeka images not in his collection. Upon moving to the Kansas City area, Harmon became active in the Heart of America Postcard Collectors club and began attending postcard shows and sales, finding more rare views of Topeka.

In December 1999, Don created Harmon Publications, publishing his *Postcard History of Topeka*, a hardback book featuring 298 real-photo postcards of the city. Harmon marketed his book throughout several retail outlets in the Topeka area. His success with his Topeka postcard book led him to publish a second book in September 2006 titled, *A Postcard History of the Early Santa Fe Railway*. This book contains an amazing 654 color and black-and-white postcards featuring the history of the Atchison, Topeka, and Santa Fe Railroad.

In 2007, Don's wife, Joyce, passed away after the two had shared more than 50 years of marriage. Harmon decided to move to a retirement village in the Ozarks, and in addition to selling his house in Shawnee, he decided to sell his postcard collection. He had successfully published two volumes showcasing his spectacular real-photo postcards, and he decided to pass the collection on to someone else. After some negotiation, Harmon decided to sell both his Topeka card collection and his Santa Fe card collection to fellow postcard collector and dealer Henry Heflin. Heflin has sold some of the collection and has the remainder for sale.

Don Harmon's love for the Topeka he knew as a boy grew into a hobby that he shared with the world through the publication of his two books. As a fellow author and historic photograph enthusiast, I was impressed with Harmon's graciousness, his generosity, and his enthusiasm for Topeka photographs. I feel honored to share some of his cards in this publication.

This real-photo postcard looks to the northwest at the 800 block of Kansas Avenue, taken from the corner at Ninth Street. Notice that the streetcars traveled down the center of the avenue, while horse traffic traveled on both sides. When this photograph was taken around 1908, this block of Kansas Avenue had not yet been paved with brick. (Courtesy Don Harmon.)

This postcard view is of the east side of the 500 block of Kansas Avenue around 1908. The building at the far right is Capitol Building and Loan Association's first building. The avenue had fully transitioned from frame to masonry buildings, with only one wooden structure that remained on the block, the tenth from the right in this view. An 1880 view of this block appears on page 15. (Courtesy Don Harmon.)

Kansas Avenue had become metropolitan in this 1908 image. This photograph looks north from Tenth Avenue. From this point one can see the F. H. Schafer Café, 929 Kansas Avenue; H. C. Lang Wallpaper, 908 Kansas Avenue; the City Hand Laundry, 927 Kansas Avenue; and Kiehl Laundry, 922 Kansas Avenue. Notice that there are two lanes for streetcars, as well as two traffic lanes and parallel parking for buggies and cars. (Courtesy Don Harmon.)

This view of the northeast corner of Kansas and Sixth Avenues predates the photograph on the bottom of page 57. The Capitol Building and Loan Association building can be seen in the center of the photograph. Notice that the Hub Clothing Store had been replaced with a new building by 1908. The Eells Hotel, seen here, had a new name, the Oxford. Notice the sign for Burghart's Favorite cigar (see page 20). (Courtesy Greg Hoots.)

This view of the west side of the 600 block of Kansas Avenue, taken around 1909, reveals it to be bustling with business activity. From the far left on Kansas Avenue one can see the National Hotel (635), Felix and Sons clothing and shoes (629–631), F. W. Woolworth (627), Hall Stationery (623), Western Union Telegraph (621), Crockett's Clothing (619), Flad Drugs (607), and the State Savings Bank (601). (Courtesy Special Collections, TSCPL.)

This 1912 view of snow piled on Kansas Avenue illustrates the difficulty that downtown businesses experienced after a heavy snowfall. Snow removed from the streetcar tracks in the center of the street was piled in front of businesses, including A. W. Vogel Cleaning Works, 818 Kansas Avenue; C. A. Karlan Furniture Company, 822 Kansas Avenue; C. M. Hill and Company wallpaper, 826 Kansas Avenue; and Coe Brothers picture framing, 828 Kansas Avenue. (Courtesy Special Collections, TSCPL.)

As a result of the popularity of real-photo postcards, the 1908 flood became the most-photographed disaster of its time in Topeka. Images of the floodwaters abound. This view, looking to the west on Crane Street from Madison Street, shows the degree of flooding experienced in the bottoms. As a point of reference, Hills Pet Food factory, located at 320 Northeast Crane Street, is located today where the houses are seen in this photograph. (Courtesy Don Harmon.)

North Topeka was heavily damaged by the 1908 flood, a much photographed disaster. In this view of North Kansas Avenue, five men ride down the street in a boat, while another is knee deep in water. The building with the tower to the right is Fire Station No. 1, located at 930 North Kansas Avenue. Compare this to the 1903 flood view on page 111. (Courtesy Special Collections, TSCPL.)

60

The Copeland Hotel, located at the southeast corner of Ninth Street and Kansas Avenue, just one block from the statehouse, was home for many members of the legislature. The hotel burned on January 14, 1909, suffering a complete loss, as well as one death and many injuries from guests jumping from windows. Notice that large power poles were placed against one wall to prevent the building's collapse into the street. (Courtesy Special Collections, TSCPL.)

The Chesterfield Hotel was located at 113 Kansas Avenue next to the Rock Island Railroad depot. Built in 1889 by W. A. Sells, the hotel catered to traveling salesmen with display room for their products. Though the hotel survived a 1921 fire, it would succumb to demolition in 1965 to make room for a parking lot. (Courtesy Special Collections, TSCPL.)

The Rock Island Railroad depot (above) was built in 1887 on the west side of Kansas Avenue at First Avenue. Notice that the Chesterfield Hotel was located next door, south of the depot. Limestone for the construction on this building was obtained from a Rock Island quarry west of Alma, Kansas, and was transported by rail to Topeka. The depot was demolished in 1943. (Courtesy Don Harmon.)

A westbound passenger train backs into the Topeka Rock Island depot. The Rock Island line used Union Pacific tracks from Kansas City to Topeka, and because of the location of the depot, westbound trains had to back into the station. The round-trip fare between Topeka and St. Louis on the Rock Island line was $9.20 in 1900. (Courtesy Greg Hoots.)

Delivery wagons for Stone Produce Company are parked in front of the 526 North Kansas Avenue building. This view of the wholesale produce enterprise was taken around 1908. In the 1910s, Allyn Stone moved his produce business to 128 Kansas Avenue. In an interesting twist, Stone sold his business in the early 1920s to Eddie Morris, and immediately after the repeal of Prohibition, Stone Produce became a wholesale liquor distributorship. (Courtesy Don Harmon.)

The Union Pacific Railroad was the first to reach Topeka, and it constructed the first depot in North Topeka in 1866. That wooden depot was replaced with this brick one, located on the east side of North Kansas Avenue, south of the tracks. This depot was home to the Palace Hotel. The railroad's decision to place the depot north of the river prompted the city to bridge the Kansas River. (Courtesy Special Collections, TSCPL.)

This December 6, 1907, Wolcott photograph shows a crowd gathered as firemen battle a blaze at Rice Hall at Washburn University. The fire gutted the building, causing $31,000 in damage, yet amazingly, it was successfully repaired. On June 8, 1966, the hall was struck by a tornado, destroying it. Completed in 1874 at a cost of $60,000, Rice Hall was one of the first buildings at the new campus. (Courtesy Special Collections, TSCPL.)

The First Baptist Church of Topeka was founded on March 1, 1857. This church building was constructed at the northeast corner of Ninth and Jackson Streets in 1870–1871. The church was one of the finest buildings in the city when completed, and its distinctive dome can be seen in many photographs of downtown. Notice the church's spire can be seen behind the Daily Capital building on the opposite page. (Courtesy Special Collections, TSCPL.)

The new Topeka State Journal building was constructed on the southeast corner of Eighth and Kansas Avenues in 1914, on the site of the old State Journal building (see page 23). The newspaper was purchased in 1885 by Frank P. MacLennan, who owned the paper until it was purchased by Oscar S. Stauffer in 1940. In 1956, Stauffer Publications purchased the *Daily Capital* and created the *Topeka Capital-Journal* in 1981. (Courtesy Don Harmon.)

The Topeka Daily Capital building, constructed in 1908, was located at the southeast corner of Eighth Avenue and Jackson Street. The *Capital*, originally at the southwest corner of Eighth Avenue and Quincy Street, was founded in 1879 by Maj. J. K. Hudson and had the first electric motor press in the country. Arthur Capper's family purchased the paper in 1901, and he purchased the partners' stock in 1904, becoming the sole owner. (Courtesy Greg Hoots.)

This Harold B. Wolfe real-photo postcard shows the southwest corner of Eighth Avenue and Quincy Street. Across the skyline are, from left to right, the Hotel Kansan; the Atchison, Topeka, and Santa Fe Railroad office; the First Baptist Church; and the state capitol building. This postcard is dated 1928. Wolfe's first camera as a professional photographer was a postcard camera, which produced this image. (Courtesy Greg Hoots.)

The Church of the Assumption is the oldest Catholic parish in Topeka. It was organized in 1862. There have been three churches built on this site at 208 West Eighth Avenue. The one pictured here was constructed in 1924. To the far right one can see the Capital Catholic High School, which would later be known as Hayden High School, now located at 401 Gage Boulevard. (Courtesy Special Collections, TSCPL.)

This view of the Security Benefit Association's tower building was taken around 1930, shortly after its completion. This structure, designed to resemble Independence Hall, was built in stages from 1924 to 1930. The Security Benefit Association was a fraternal organization with the goal of providing medical and long-term care for orphans and the aged. Menninger Foundation purchased the property in the 1960s, operating a psychiatric hospital there until moving in 2003. (Courtesy Greg Hoots.)

The new Bank of Topeka building, owned by John and Joab Mulvane, was constructed at the northwest corner of Sixth and Kansas Avenues and was completed in 1907, as seen above. Only 25 years later, this building was razed, and a new, larger building was constructed on the site (see page 73). John R. Mulvane served as president of the Bank of Topeka from 1879 until his death in 1918. (Courtesy Don Harmon.)

THE FLYING ROOSTER

This real-photo postcard from the 1940s shows the *Flying Rooster*, an airplane owned by radio station WIBW and Capper Publications. In this view, the aircraft sits on a snowy airfield. The station purchased a second, larger airplane, also dubbed, the *Flying Rooster*, but tragedy struck that aircraft on April 20, 1949, when it crashed en route to western Kansas, killing the pilot and staff members onboard. (Courtesy Greg Hoots.)

NOTHING ESCAPED THE FURY OF THE TORNADO

As an example of the media material produced after the June 8, 1966, tornado, more than 100 real-photo postcard views of the tornado and its destruction were marketed in Topeka after the storm. Produced by an unknown and unlisted publisher, the cards like the one above show the devastating toll of the storm. Everyone with a camera in Topeka became a photographer on June 9. (Courtesy Greg Hoots.)

Three

HAROLD B. WOLFE'S TOPEKA

Born in Havensville, Kansas, in 1898, Harold B. Wolfe came to Topeka in 1916 looking for work. His first job was at Banner Lunch, located at 623 Kansas Avenue, as a dishwasher. His job was a 12-hour shift of tiring, tedious work scrubbing pots, pans, and dishes without respite. He was paid $4 a week and meals—$1.25 a week of that he spent on his room. He left Topeka in 1918 to return to Havensville, as his name had been called for the military draft. Before he was to report, however, the war ended, and he was never called to service. Wolfe returned to Topeka and did various jobs as a salesman and had a brief stint with the *Daily Capital* in the advertising department. In 1923, Wolfe found himself working in the office at Standard Oil Company. While attending a company picnic, he noticed that photographs were being taken, and as his sister had a darkroom kit, he offered to print extra photographs for employees.

Wolfe realized that the photography business was something he enjoyed and for which he had great talent. A friend, Jesse Wright, who owned a photo-finishing business, gave Wolfe a folding Kodak postcard camera. Introduced in 1903 by Kodak, the postcard camera produced a negative that was the size of a penny postcard, and the image could be transferred to a postcard blank by means of a contact print. Wolfe began his career as a photographer with that camera. In 1924, Wolfe quit his job with Standard Oil and opened his first photography store at 826 Kansas Avenue. In 1926, he moved his store to 720 Kansas Avenue and, in 1928, moved to 631 Jackson Street, where he remained for more than 25 years. In 1951, Wolfe opened a store at 915 North Kansas Avenue (see page 71). In 1953, the downtown store was moved from Jackson Street to 106 West Eighth Street, while a new store opened at 2017 Gage Boulevard in 1955.

In 1946, Wolfe's brother-in-law, Harold Worswick, went to work for Wolfe at his Jackson Street store. In 1954, Worswick became a partner in the photography business as the new stores were being opened in Topeka. Early in the 1960s, Worswick purchased the Wolfe's Camera business from his brother-in-law, as Wolfe contemplated retirement. However, retirement was not agreeable to Wolfe, and he and his sons, Dick and Jack, opened a small camera shop and photography business in Holiday Square at Twenty-ninth Street and Topeka Boulevard. Wolfe continued to take commercial photography jobs and work in the store until his death from a heart attack in October 1966.

Harold Wolfe had two great loves in his life, photography and his family. In September 1925, Wolfe married Mary Margaret Miller, and the couple had four sons, Harold Jr., Bob, Jack, and Dick. As boys, Wolfe put his sons to work at his shops, and he greatly enjoyed working with them. The first Christmas after Harold Jr. was born, Wolfe created a Christmas card to send to friends that featured a photograph of their son. This began a long tradition of producing Christmas or New Years cards that featured photographs of his four sons, "the Wolfe Cubs." For 10 years during the Depression, the cards were thematic, expressing the seriousness of the economic climate and hope for the future. After his boys were grown and had families, they, too, sent Christmas cards featuring photographs of their families. Wolfe, then, would take those images and create a New Years card to send back to them all.

Wolfe's professional work was unparalleled by any other photographer of his time. Early in his career, Wolfe came to the conclusion that commercial photography for businesses, government agencies, and schools showed great promise as a source of work. He acquired a large-format camera that used sheets of film that were 8 by 10 inches in size and produced extremely clear and sharp images. Wolfe used this camera throughout his career, long after most photographers had switched to smaller, less cumbersome equipment. His decision to continue to use the large-format camera was reflected in the quality of his photographic images.

Nancy Sherbert, curator of photographs for the Kansas State Archives, remarked that she could recognize a Wolfe photograph without ever seeing his stamp on the reverse or his WOLFE signature on the image. His photographic style and the quality of his images make his work easily recognizable. The sheer size of his prints grabs the eye. The sharpness of the detail and the seemingly perfect camera angle are also Wolfe trademarks.

During the Depression, Harold Wolfe looked for new opportunities in commercial photography to offset the loss of business due to the economic crisis. Wolfe photographed all of the public works projects for city, state, and federal government agencies. In 1932, Wolfe was commissioned by the Topeka Commercial Club to photograph most Topeka businesses for a large scrapbook that it was creating to promote the city. It was during this time that Wolfe created his panorama photographs of Kansas Avenue. From atop buildings, he photographed Kansas Avenue businesses in long, stretched images. The commercial club and the panorama photographs are part of the collection at the Kansas State Archives and can be viewed there. A collection of Wolfe photographs is also available for viewing at the Kansas State Historical Society's Web site, Kansasmemory.org.

Harold Wolfe was also well known as a school photographer, taking class photographs, sports photographs, and event photography. On one of Wolfe's postcards advertising his school services was the motto, "Every Saturday is teachers day at Wolfe's."

No photographer in the history of Topeka produced more images of the city than Harold B. Wolfe. An individual could collect nothing but Wolfe images and fill a room. There are few people in the history of the city of Topeka who have done more to preserve its history than Harold Wolfe. It is easy to argue, in fact, that he is among the greatest Topeka historians, chronicling five decades, yet he never wrote a word.

Thousands of negatives from Wolfe's work were lost during the move from 631 Jackson Street, a grievous loss for all Kansas historians. However, a plentitude of Wolfe images exist, a tribute to his dedication to photography and his trade.

Today Wolfe's Camera still bears its founder's name and is located just a block from the location of the old Jackson Street store. Located in the new Kresge building at 635 Kansas Avenue, Wolfe's Camera has been an icon in downtown Topeka for more than 85 years.

Above, Harold B. Wolfe talks to a customer at the camera shop that he shared with his sons in the Holiday Square shopping center. Wolfe and his sons opened the store after the elder Wolfe sold his interest in Wolfe Camera to his brother-in-law, Harold Worswick. Wolfe worked from the Holiday Square store until his death in 1966. (Courtesy Susan Wolfe.)

Wolfe's Camera opened a North Topeka store in the fall of 1951. Located at 915 North Kansas Avenue, Wolfe's shared the building with Hess Jewelry, divided by a center wall. Similarly, the main store at 631 Jackson Street only had 8 feet of storefront. Jack Wolfe can be seen in the window of the store. (Courtesy Susan Wolfe.)

Harold and Mary Wolfe's four sons, from left to right, Dick, Jack, Robert, and Harold Jr., pose for this 1938 New Years Card. The card featured images of the six previous years' cards, each featuring a Depression-era theme. Notice the elaborate props that Wolfe prepared for his annual holiday card. (Courtesy Susan Wolfe.)

In 1939, as the Works Progress Administration (WPA) programs were nearing completion at Gage Park, Harold Wolfe photographed their accomplishments for the City of Topeka. Above, a pony wagon contains seven ponies and two burros, all saddled and ready for young riders at the park. Other improvements at the park included the swimming pool, new roads, and new tennis courts (see page 115). (Courtesy Special Collections, TSCPL.)

The National Bank of Topeka moved into a new building at 535 Kansas Avenue (above) in 1932. Originally founded as the Topeka Bank and Savings Institution in 1868, the bank was moved from 501 Kansas Avenue to 601 Kansas Avenue in the early 1870s. In 1883, the bank was moved into John and Joab Mulvane's bank building at 535 Kansas Avenue. In 1907, that building was razed, and the new Mulvane building was constructed for the bank (see page 67). In 1931, the second Mulvane building was razed, and construction began on the building seen above. Designed by architect Thomas Williamson, the building was considered to be a modern skyscraper, equipped with high-speed elevators and air-conditioning. The building was imploded on June 18, 1995 (see inset). (Courtesy Kansas State Historical Society; inset photograph courtesy of Greg Hoots.)

Crane and Company, a longtime business in Topeka, seen above in the Thatcher building, was founded as Crane and Bryon in 1868. The business suffered two devastating fires before dissolving in 1873. Crane continued in the printing business alone, surviving yet another fire before incorporating and moving to 110 East Eighth Avenue in 1899. This Harold B. Wolfe photograph dates to the early 1930s. (Courtesy Kansas State Historical Society.)

The new Union Pacific Railroad station, located at 701 North Kansas Avenue, can be seen here at its opening in 1927. The building, designed by Gilbert Stanley Underwood, was among the most elegant railroad stations in the state. The station closed in 1971, and in 1998, the Union Pacific donated the property to Topeka Railroad Days, Inc. The station has been converted into a museum, education center, and veterans' memorial. (Courtesy Kansas State Historical Society.)

This Harold B. Wolfe photograph shows the Union Bus Station, located at 107 West Sixth Avenue, in what is known as the Stormont Building. Designed to be 10 stories tall, the first two floors were completed in 1926, but the remaining floors were never completed. For 25 years, J.C. Penny's store was located here. In 1927, Davis-Wellcome Mortgage, Union News Company Sandwich Shop, and Dawson Real Estate were located here. (Courtesy Kansas State Historical Society.)

Holt and Son Tire Company and gas station at 1001 Quincy Street is seen in this Harold B. Wolfe photograph taken in the 1930s. Notice the White Eagle gasoline eagles mounted on top of the pumps and the larger eagle at the sidewalk. Virtually every business that existed in Topeka in 1940 was captured on film by Wolfe. (Courtesy Kansas State Historical Society.)

This 1928 Harold Wolfe photograph shows the Gem Market delivery trucks parked in front of the Gem Market and the Gem Drug Store, located at 506 West Tenth Avenue. Identified seated in the trucks are, from left to right, ? Willard, Tom Speck, Bud Leuenberger, and Clarence C., while the man on the sidewalk at right is listed as a Mr. McKenna. (Courtesy Kansas State Historical Society.)

The Hotel Kansan, constructed in 1923 (see page 43), can be seen in this Harold B. Wolfe real-photo postcard from the 1930s. The hotel faces Ninth Street at the northeast corner of Kansas Avenue. In 1968, the hotel closed and was converted into an 88-unit apartment building, with business suites on the ground floor. (Courtesy Special Collections, TSCPL.)

The Columbian Building, located at 112–114 West Sixth Avenue, was built during the 1888 construction boom in Topeka. Designed by architect Seymour Davis, the building has extensive ornate decorations adorning both the exterior and interior. The five-story building was constructed for businessman William C. Knox, who operated his U.S. Savings Bank there until 1892, when Columbian Title and Trust and Columbian Securities moved into the building. This Harold B. Wolfe view dates from the early 1930s. The building was renovated and placed on the National Register of Historic Buildings in 1975. Another view of the building can be seen at the top of page 34. (Courtesy Kansas State Historical Society.)

Above, the Central National Bank building, located at 701 Kansas Avenue, was completed in April 1927. The architectural firm of Wright and Wright of Kansas City designed the building, which was imposing and opulent, both inside and out. Pictured at left, Capitol Building and Loan Association constructed this skyscraper in 1923 at 534 Kansas Avenue. Designed by George Elmslie, the building featured the sculpture named *Kansas Family*, presented in relief over the front door. Lost for years after the building's demolition in 1968, the sculpture was discovered dumped in Gage Park in 1994. Its restoration was financed by Capitol Federal Savings and Loan, and it was then installed in the Helen Hocker Theater in Gage Park. (Both, courtesy Kansas State Historical Society.)

Above, Joseph Hoover shows off his parade car, a 1904 Reo, for the boys at Hoover Drug Store, located at the southwest corner of Tenth and Kansas Avenues, in this 1930s Harold B. Wolfe photograph. At right, the Jayhawk Hotel, located at 700 Jackson Street, was built in 1926, to fill the need left by the closing of the National Hotel at 635 Kansas Avenue. The Jayhawk had 300 rooms, with a capacity of 1,200, and many state legislators stayed at the hotel when the legislature was in session. (Above, courtesy Lloyd Zimmer; right, courtesy Kansas State Historical Society.)

Harold B. Wolfe produced a series of panoramic photographs of businesses on Kansas Avenue in the 1930s. The entire collection of images is available for viewing at the state archives. Above, businesses on the east side of the 600 block of Kansas Avenue included the Fair Store, David J.

August, Banner Lunch, Frank Furniture Company, Acme Quality Paint, Nygren Brothers Tailors, Christopher Studio, Stansfield Drug Company, and C. E. Warden and Sons. (Courtesy Kansas State Historical Society.)

Wolfe's commercial photography business chronicled the achievements of the various public works projects that were undertaken during the Great Depression. Above, the Topeka Water Department facility, located at the north end of MacVicar Avenue, is photographed upon completion in 1939. Wolfe photographed many projects, including Phillip Billard Airport, Gage Park improvements, three new fire stations, and the new police station. (Courtesy Special Collections, TSCPL.)

The new Topeka Police Station, seen above, was a Public Works Administration project that was completed in 1937. The building was located on the northwest corner of Fifth and Jackson Streets. In 1994, Topeka voters approved a sales tax to finance a new Law Center at Fourth Street and Kansas Avenue. The police station pictured above was demolished and replaced with parking. (Courtesy Special Collections, TSCPL.)

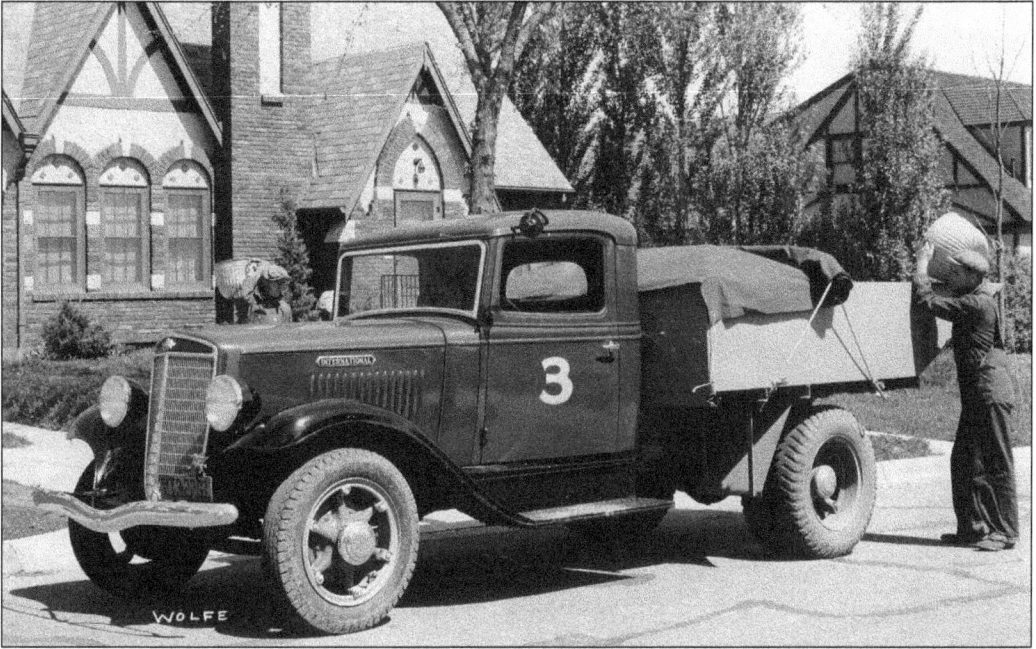

One of the public works projects initiated in Topeka during the Great Depression was the creation of the county's solid waste disposal program. Garbage collectors can be seen loading trash into the back of a 1935 International truck at a Collins Park residence in this 1938 Harold B. Wolfe photograph. (Courtesy Special Collections, TSCPL.)

Among the public works projects completed in Topeka during the Great Depression were the construction of three new fire stations, including this station, No. 7, located at 1215 Southwest Oakley Avenue. A Topeka Fire Department fire truck is seen parked in front of the station in this Harold B. Wolfe photograph, taken around 1936. (Courtesy Special Collections, TSCPL.)

At 10 stories tall, for several years the National Reserve Life insurance building, located at the southeast corner of Tenth and Kansas Avenues, was Topeka's tallest building. This 1927 view of the building is one of Harold B. Wolfe's classic nighttime photographs. Completed in 1925, the National Reserve Building was hit by the devastating June 8, 1966, tornado and was severely damaged. The entire building was refaced and remodeled, and became an apartment building. This photograph, as all of Wolfe's commercial photographs, was taken with a large-format camera using film that was 8 by 10 inches in size, producing incredibly sharp images. (Courtesy Lloyd Zimmer.)

The Star Shoe Shop, located at 106 West Seventeenth Street, is seen in this Harold Wolfe photograph from the 1930s. A deliveryman, seated on a three-wheeled Harley Davidson motorcycle, seems very official decked out in his uniform, complete with tie. Notice that Seventeenth Street was paved with bricks. (Courtesy Lloyd Zimmer.)

This 1930 photograph, taken by Harold Wolfe from the northwest corner of Tenth and Kansas Avenues looking south, is one of Wolfe's many night scene photographs taken for commercial businesses. On the east side of the avenue one can see Montgomery Ward, located at 912 Kansas Avenue, Karlan Furniture at 900 Kansas Avenue, and the towering columns of the Hotel Kansas on the north side of Ninth Street. (Courtesy Lloyd Zimmer.)

The Novelty Vaudeville Theater, seen here in a 1926 Wolfe photograph, was located at the northwest corner of Eighth Avenue and Quincy Street. Built in 1896, the theater offered both vaudeville and dramatic productions. At the time of this image, the theater offered only live performances; motion pictures were introduced to this theater in 1929. (Courtesy Kansas State Historical Society.)

The Grand Theater, located at 615 Jackson Street, was constructed in 1882, opening as Topeka Opera House. By the late 1920s, movies had become the common fare at the Grand, as with most of the early opera houses. This Wolfe photograph was taken in 1933 when the popular movie *King Kong* was showing. (Courtesy Kansas State Historical Society.)

Four

TOPEKA FREE FAIR

In 1870, when the state of Kansas was less than a decade old, A. J. Ryan donated 24 acres of land to the City of Topeka for a fairgrounds and added 8 more acres in 1871, the year of the first fair held in the city. State fairs had been held in Lawrence, Fort Scott, and Leavenworth in the late 1860s and early 1870s, but no permanent state fairgrounds existed. In 1881, the Kansas State Fair Association was formed, and 48 acres were added to the Topeka fairgrounds, making its total area of 80 acres. The association would host the state fair in Topeka from 1881 through 1883 and again from 1886 through 1893. In 1902, the Kansas State Fair Association entered into a 10-year lease of the Topeka fairgrounds and began holding the state fair there annually.

In 1913, Hutchinson state senator Emerson Carey and his political allies were successful in having the Central Kansas Fair, which was held annually in Hutchinson, designated as the official state fair of Kansas. The legislation would give the fairgrounds property in Hutchinson to the state in exchange for financial support for the fair and for the right to exclusively use the name "the Kansas State Fair." Carey had made the legislative proposal every year for some time, having the bill pass in the Senate and fail in the House of Representatives. In 1913, however, there was a rift in the state Republican Party, and through some political shenanigans, the bill passed both houses and became law, moving the state fair to Hutchinson.

Fair planners in Topeka were irate. The 1913 and 1914 fairs were still held at the fairgrounds as before, but the lack of the recognizable designation as the state fair bothered organizers. So, in 1915, the fair in Topeka was renamed the Kansas Free Fair, and the admission charge was eliminated. The 1915 fair was a moderate success, with an attendance of 200,000.

Fair attendance continued to rise throughout the 1920s and 1930s before peaking in 1948, with an attendance record of 506,000. With such a record of growth and success, the fair board was unpleasantly surprised when gate attendance dropped almost in half in 1951, and then, when rain persisted during fair week in 1952, only 125,000 attended. The fair was consistently losing money, a bill that the county was obligated to pay. Attendance improved in the late 1950s, with 1958 attendance set at 409,500. Despite the improvement, the fair continued to sustain financial losses, so a decision was made to end the Kansas Free Fair after 1958.

In 1959, the county entered into a 10-year lease with the Mid-America Fair Association to host the fair in Topeka under the new name Mid-America Fair. A gate charge of 50¢ for adults, with children admitted free, was instituted. The fair board noted that it was the same gate admission charge that was collected at the fair in 1883. Despite the admission charge, the fair's numbers improved in 1959, with 411,000 in attendance.

As the 1960s progressed, the fair saw dwindling crowds and fewer sponsoring exhibitors. The fairgrounds buildings were also deteriorating, and in 1974, the county commission severed the lease of the fairgrounds with the Mid-America Fair Association. In 1975, the fair carried a new name, the Sunflower State Expo. There was some uncertainty among commissioners as to what they should do with the fairgrounds, and in 1976, the Shawnee County Fair Advisory Board was created, and fairs continued to be held. A number of commissioners favored closing the fairgrounds and developing the land for another use, such as a civic center. As no decision had been made, the 1980 Sunflower State Expo opened in September with a new feature—free admission. Attendance had been only 55,000 in 1979, and the fair board was desperate to attract larger crowds.

For decades, the racetrack at the fairgrounds had been leased to automobile racing promoters, who held races at the track every Saturday night and often on summer holidays. The racing concession was virtually the only income that the fair board had, exclusive of fair week. On July 4, 1980, in the morning, prior to a scheduled Independence Day race at the fairgrounds, a small tornado ripped through central Topeka, striking the grandstand, causing large chunks of the concrete roof to fall into the seating area. Fortunately, there were no fans in the grandstand at the time; however, the race was cancelled. Commissioners feared that the structure was unsafe, and it was never used again.

Fairs continued to be held in 1980 and 1981, and then it was announced that the 1982 Sunflower State Expo would be the last fair at the Topeka fairgrounds. Attendance was 82,000, down slightly from the previous year, and the fair lost $98,405, which was paid by the Shawnee County Commission.

On April 25, 1983, Shawnee County voters approved a $19.7 million bond issue that financed the demolition of most of the fairgrounds buildings and the construction of the new Kansas Expocentre complex. The Landon Arena opened on April 17, 1987, with a sold-out concert. In 1998, the 224-room Capitol Plaza Hotel opened on the Expocentre grounds, built by developer John Q. Hammonds.

In the planning of the Expocentre, the Agricultural Hall, Livestock Pavilion and Exposition Hall, and Heritage Hall, all vestiges of the fairgrounds' past were saved and incorporated into the new convention center.

In looking at the history of the fairgrounds in Topeka, one conclusion is certain: the facility had outlived its usefulness. When the fairgrounds was created in 1870, Topeka had a population of fewer than 6,000 people. County fairs and even the state fair were products of a rural economy, and by 1920, while Topeka's population had grown to 50,022, fair attendance had grown to 350,000, with most of those attendees coming from rural parts of the state. As Topeka became more and more urban and Kansas became less populated in its rural areas, the appeal of the fair in Topeka diminished.

If the Kansas State Fair had remained in Topeka, rather than moving to Hutchinson in 1913, it is quite likely that the event would still be held annually at fairgrounds at Seventeenth Street and Topeka Avenue. The designation and title of "State Fair" has preserved the annual event in Hutchinson, primarily because of the extensive network of county 4-H fairs that still exist across Kansas.

As for the fairgrounds in Topeka, the Kansas Expocentre has flourished, providing new life to a section of the city that had fallen into disrepair. Fortunately, many memories and many photographs remain of the Kansas Free Fair in Topeka.

This etching of the state fairgrounds in Topeka was created by Henry Worrall in 1871 and shows the fairgrounds in its infancy. Notice at the far right that an Atchison, Topeka, and Santa Fe railroad spur line runs into the fairgrounds from the east, entering at about Eighteenth Street. Topeka can be seen in the distance to the north. (Courtesy Kansas State Historical Society.)

This view of the state fairgrounds in Topeka, dated 1881, looks to the east. At the far left one can see the tents of the midway. The grandstands, left of center, are full, and hundreds of wagons and horses are in the infield of the racetrack. The houses in the background are located on Topeka Boulevard. In 1881, there were no houses between the fairgrounds and Washburn University. (Courtesy Kansas State Historical Society.)

In this view of the carnival midway at the Topeka fairgrounds one can see the Ferris wheel and carousel to the right and a row of vendor tents to the left. This view of the fair is from 1915, the first year of the Kansas Free Fair, after the state fair was moved to Hutchinson. Attendance for the 1915 Kansas Free Fair is listed at 200,000. (Courtesy Kansas State Historical Society.)

The Topeka Railway Company operated streetcars for carrying passengers to the fairgrounds in Topeka. Insofar as daily attendance at early fairs would sometimes exceed 40,000, transportation for fairgoers was important. The streetcar line ran to the northeast corner of the fairgrounds, with a small station near the main gate. After World War II, the automobile became the preferred transportation to the fairgrounds. (Courtesy Kansas State Historical Society.)

This photograph of the midway at the Kansas Free Fair dates from 1917. Visible in the center of the image is the House of Capper. The facility, provided by Arthur Capper's publishing company, made drinking water and restrooms available to the public at the fair. The building was located at the far north end of the fairgrounds. It can be located on the map of the fairgrounds on page 96. (Courtesy Kansas State Historical Society.)

This display at the 1924 Kansas Free Fair was produced by the Kansas Automobile Owners Association and the Kansas Highway Commission. Located under the new grandstand, the display showed Kansas' poor record for construction of "365 day roads" and promoted the idea of a network of paved highways for the state. In 1924, there were only a handful of paved roads in Kansas. (Courtesy Kansas State Historical Society.)

Above, Stinson Day during fair week in 1917 drew a record crowd of more than 15,000 to watch Katherine Stinson, called the "Flying Schoolgirl," perform an aerial exhibition. Stinson was touring the country in 1917 raising money for the American Red Cross. Notice the Curtiss Stinson-Special aircraft in the infield of the fairgrounds racetrack. The airplane was a specially prepared Curtiss JN-4D "Jenny" modified with a single seat. Shown at left, Katherine Stinson stands next to her airplane in the infield at the Topeka fairgrounds. Stinson retired from flying at the end of 1917 to become an ambulance driver for the American Red Cross in Europe during the war. Stinson was the first woman to perform a flying loop, performing the maneuver more than 500 times. She was also the first woman to carry the U.S. Air Mail. (Both, courtesy Kansas State Historical Society.)

Auto racing began at the fairgrounds in September 1902, and soon the sport became one of the most popular events, featuring racing every week. Racing on the flat horse track required considerable skill and daring. Above, the new grandstand, constructed in 1923 at a cost of $200,000, was packed with fans in this 1924 photograph. Below, cars race down the front stretch and into turn one in this 1921 view. Racing was held at the fairgrounds until July 4, 1980, when the grandstands were struck by a tornado, severely damaging the roof, causing chunks of concrete to fall into the seating. A race was scheduled to be held later that day; it was cancelled, and no events were ever held at the grandstands or racetrack again. (Both, courtesy Kansas State Historical Society.)

Above, the original entrance to the Kansas State Fairgrounds is seen in this 1908 real-photo postcard. The entrance ran diagonally into the fairgrounds from the southwest corner of Seventeenth Street and Topeka Boulevard. Although the state fair was moved to Hutchinson in 1915, a new gate was not constructed until 1940. Notice in this view that the fire station at 1715 Topeka Avenue had not yet been constructed. (Courtesy Special Collections, TSCPL.)

This 1915 view of the midway at the Topeka fairgrounds shows the enthusiasm by the crowd for the fair. Notice along the main walk the women are wearing long white dresses, and many of the men are dressed in suits. This photograph was taken from the grandstand looking north. The fair boasted a 1-mile-long midway of sideshows, food, and games. (Courtesy Kansas State Historical Society.)

Above, the new gate and entrance for the Kansas Free Fair in Topeka were completed by the Works Progress Administration in 1940, capping seven years of construction at the fairgrounds. Public works projects funded the construction of 14 buildings at the fairgrounds during the 1930s. At right, the Memorial Tower, unveiled on September 11, 1948, was located at the Eighteenth Street entrance to the fairgrounds on Topeka Avenue. Constructed at a cost of $25,000, the tower stood 60 feet tall and was faced with porcelain panels. On its west side, 20 panels form a painting of the flag raising over Iwo Jima. Those panels are now displayed at the Combat Air Museum. (Above, courtesy Kansas State Historical Society; right, courtesy Combat Air Museum.)

This map of the Kansas Free Fair Grounds was printed in the center of the 1927 Kansas Free Fair program. Hall Topeka, a longtime printing business, provided free programs for fair attendees. The map only displays areas on the 80-acre grounds that lie north of the grandstand, including the midway and exhibition halls. In this view, the top of the map points to the north. (Courtesy Greg Hoots.)

Above, a good crowd filled the midway in this 1951 Harold B. Wolfe view from the Kansas Free Fair looking to the north. At right, this 1951 photograph by Hyland Clifton captures the timelessness of a day at the fair. The year 1951 was the beginning of the end for the Kansas Free Fair. Attendance had peaked at the fair in 1948 at 506,000, and by 1951, that number had dropped to 300,000. In 1952, things worsened, with only 125,000 in attendance, as the weather was poor. In 1959, the decision was made to charge admission to the fair, and the Kansas Free Fair was no more, with its new name being the Mid-America Fair. (Both, courtesy Kansas State Historical Society.)

An unidentified trophy girl sits in this 1963 Studebaker Lark Daytona convertible pace car at the Topeka fairgrounds offices at Eighteenth and Western Streets. Saturday night stock car racing was a staple at the fairgrounds' 1.5-mile dirt track after World War II. The last scheduled race at the fairgrounds was to be held on July 4, 1980, but the event was cancelled when a tornado struck the grandstands. Below, fireworks illuminated the sky at the fairgrounds after a day's celebration in this July 4, 1924, photograph. Fireworks were a regular fare at the racetrack, despite the fact that during a 1912 celebration such pyrotechnics caused a blaze on the roof of the old grandstand that was extinguished by "ripping out a few shingles and beating out flames," as reported in the *Topeka State Journal*. (Both, courtesy Kansas State Historical Society.)

Five

FORBES AIR FORCE BASE

In the days that followed the Japanese attack at Pearl Harbor, the United States mobilized its armed forces and its civilian workforce to a new end, winning the war. Within two weeks of the attack, the U.S. Army activated army airfields across the country, recognizing the increased importance of aviation in modern warfare. Fifteen airfields were created in the early 1940s in Kansas, including the Topeka Army Airfield, located at Pauline, a small town on the south outskirts of Topeka. The base took eight months to construct, at a cost of $10 million. The base was designed to accommodate 5,000 men and opened on August 22, 1942; however, work on the barracks was not completed when the men arrived, so soldiers were housed at the fairgrounds until their quarters were finished.

The first unit assigned to the airfield was the 333rd Bombardment Group, followed by a brief assignment by the 466th Bombardment Group. The initial assignment was to train pilots and crews for the B-24 Liberator heavy bombers. As the war progressed, the base became a staging area for Liberator crews being sent to Europe and Africa.

After the war's end, the base became headquarters for the army's Air Transport Command (ATC) in December 1945; however, that mission was a short one, and within a year the ATC division closed. By the end of 1946, most of the base's 700 aircraft had been moved, and in May 1947, the announcement came that the Topeka Army Airfield would close, leaving only a small civilian staff to maintain the grounds. By the end of 1947, the last army plane had left Topeka.

The U.S. Air Force was created on September 18, 1947, replacing the U.S. Army Air Force, and by early 1948, the air force was planning on closing some former army airfields while developing others. Early 1948 found Topeka city leaders hoping to find a new tenant for the airfield. That hope was realized when the 55th Reconnaissance Group moved to the newly designated Topeka Air Force Base from MacDill Field, Florida. By late 1948, around 4,700 airmen were stationed at the Topeka base.

On July 13, 1949, the base was renamed again, this time in honor of Maj. Daniel H. Forbes Jr., a Carbondale, Kansas, native. Forbes, a highly decorated World War II reconnaissance pilot, was killed on June 5, 1948, when he and copilot Capt. Glen Edwards crashed in the California desert while testing the Northrop YB-49 "Flying Wing," the forerunner of the B-2 bomber. Muroc Air Force Base, where the crash occurred, was renamed Edwards Air Force Base.

Ironically, only 11 days after the dedication ceremonies for Forbes Air Force Base, orders came from Washington, D.C., which inactivated the base, essentially closing the facility. By August 25, 1949, the air force had completed the clean-out of the base, leaving only 12 civilian employees behind.

In February 1951, the news came that Forbes Air Force Base would reopen yet again. This time it would be home to the air force's 21st Air Division, composed of the 55th and the 90th Strategic Reconnaissance Wings and the 815th Air Base Group. While the 21st Division initially used RB-29 and RB-50 aircraft, in 1951, both wings would begin to fly the new RB-47, based on the Boeing B-47 Stratojet platform, a cold war–era medium-range bomber converted for espionage.

As Forbes Field grew with the presence of the Strategic Air Command, the need for additional housing on the base was addressed in 1957 when the air force began construction of the Capehart housing development on the southwest edge of the facility. In all, 1,054 houses were constructed at a cost of more than $16 million. The first residents of the housing development moved into their home on February 17, 1958. On January 31, 1959, the Capehart housing area would be renamed Cullen Village, after Brig. Gen. Paul T. Cullen, division commander of the 311th Air Division. The air force also constructed an elementary school to serve 450 students and built a new 100-bed hospital at a cost of $3.5 million.

On April 22, 1959, the air force announced that the 548th Strategic Missile Squadron would activate at Forbes Air Force Base, as it became home to nine intercontinental ballistic missiles. Ground-breaking ceremonies were held at the Burlington/Waverly site in June 1959, and the 548th stood up on July 1, 1960. Topeka embraced the missile program; Atlas missiles were displayed in the city prior to activation. On August 23, 1960, the public was invited to Gage Shopping Center to watch the Topeka Fire Department wash one of the missiles. The air force accepted the nine sites from the civilian contractors on July 28, 1961, and the missiles were installed almost immediately. The Atlas E missile, which was used in all nine sites, was virtually obsolete by the time it was installed. Replaced by the Atlas F, which was stored in a vertical silo, and the new Titan II and Minutemen missile systems, the Atlas E's at Forbes Air Force Base were deactivated and removed in January 1965, and the 548th Strategic Missile Squadron stood down on March 25, 1965.

By 1961, Forbes Air Force Base had become the most powerful air force installation in the world; it being the only base with the combination of a strategic reconnaissance wing (the 90th), a bombardment wing (the 40th), and an operational missile unit (the 548th). In 1961, the base led the Strategic Air Command in flying hours. In 1960, the 90th Air Refueling Squadron moved to Forbes, serving the 90th and 40th wings.

In 1965, the Strategic Air Command closed its operations at Forbes and moved much of that work to Offutt Air Force Base in Omaha. On July 1, 1965, the base was turned over to the Tactical Air Command (TAC). TAC's 838th Division operated at Forbes until its deactivation on December 24, 1969, while the 313th Tactical Airlift wing remained at Forbes until September 30, 1973, when Forbes Air Force Base closed for the last time.

In January 1974, the Metropolitan Topeka Airport Authority was created to manage the transition of the property from the U.S. Air Force to the City of Topeka. In April 1976, title was transferred to the city for 3,000 acres of property that would be transformed into a public airport and industrial park. Approximately 215 acres at the south end of the flight line were given to the Kansas Air National Guard for a permanent home for the 190th Air Refueling Wing. Today Forbes Field is a thriving business park as well as a modern airport. It is also the home of two museums, the Combat Air Museum and the Museum of the Kansas National Guard.

The history of the base was a story of feast and famine. Closed three times and operating under three names, Forbes Air Force Base played an important role in the history of Topeka and the world.

The main gate at Forbes Air Force Base is seen in this 1950s photograph. The gate was located inside the main entrance on U.S. Highway 75, or Topeka Boulevard. More than a dozen U.S. Air Force and Army Air Force units called the airfield home between 1942 and 1973. Units of the Strategic Air Command operated at Forbes from 1948 through 1964. (Courtesy Kansas State Historical Society.)

This RB-47E, a B-47 bomber converted for reconnaissance duty by the air force, sits on the apron just outside the base operations build. The "Base Ops" building was converted to the passenger airline terminal when the Topeka Metropolitan Airport Authority acquired the base in 1976. In 1985, the building was razed and replaced with a new passenger terminal. Both the 90th and 55th Strategic Reconnaissance Wings operated at the base. (Courtesy Kansas State Historical Society.)

A group of ladies tours the Base Exchange (BX) at the Topeka Army Air Field in this 1943 photograph. During the war years, some wives lived off base with their husbands in trailers near the base or in other housing in Topeka. A new BX was constructed in 1958 when 1,054 new homes for airmen's families were constructed in the Capehart housing area, later named Cullen Village. (Courtesy Kansas State Historical Society.)

This photograph, taken from the control tower at the Base Operations building, dates from 1943–1944 at the Topeka Army Air Field. Rows of B-24 Liberator heavy bombers are readied for duty overseas. The darker aircraft in the foreground were headed to Europe, while the lighter-colored airplanes in the background were destined for Africa. The base trained pilots and crews, and served as a staging area for overseas-bound aircraft. (Courtesy Combat Air Museum.)

The night refueling of a C-54 Skymaster at the Topeka Army Air Force Base was captured in this October 13, 1943, photograph. At the far right on the apron one can see the nose of a Curtiss-Wright C-46 Commando. Prior to the creation of the U.S. Air Force, this aircraft was operated by the army's Air Transport Command. The Air Transport Command was headquartered in Topeka for a short time in 1946. (Courtesy Kansas State Historical Society.)

Hattie Forbes, mother of Maj. Daniel H. Forbes, stands with U.S. Air Force officers and hundreds of airmen as they pay tribute to her son, who lost his life on June 5, 1948, while flying an experimental Northrop YB-49 Flying Wing. This ceremony, on July 16, 1949, honored Forbes by renaming the Topeka airfield Forbes Air Force Base. (Courtesy Combat Air Museum.)

A crowd gathers on the flight line apron for an Armed Forces Day parade in May 1958. To the right, a crowd inspects a F9F Cougar navy fighter and a U.S. Army H21 Shawnee helicopter. Armed Forces Day celebrations were gala events at Forbes Air Force Base, with thousands in attendance. Notice the 1958 Chevrolet convertible at the lower left; it appears to be readying itself for the parade. (Courtesy Kansas State Historical Society.)

An RB-29, a reconnaissance version of the B-29 Superfortress, is seen at the far right of this photograph, while RB-50s are parked down the flight line to the left in this 1959 image from Forbes Air Force Base. These aircraft belonged to the 90th and 55th Strategic Reconnaissance Wings of the U.S Air Force's 21st Air Division. The converted bombers were equipped with cameras designed to photograph from high altitudes. (Courtesy Kansas State Historical Society.)

Above, airmen perform air traffic control tasks from the original control tower, which was attached to the south end of the Base Operations building. From 1959 to 1965, Forbes Air Force Base was the most powerful air base in the world, leading the Strategic Air Command's bases in flying activity. Forbes logged a record 5,118 hours of flight time in July 1961. Air traffic at the base was nonstop. (Courtesy Combat Air Museum.)

A squadron of airmen is seen here marching at Forbes Air Force Base. Notice a number of the base's barracks in the background. By 1961, Forbes was the second largest air force base in the world, with more than 8,000 personnel. Forbes was virtually a city itself, on the south edge of Topeka. The base poured $5.5 million monthly into the Topeka economy in the form of salaries. (Courtesy Combat Air Museum.)

This new B-52 Stratofortress long-range bomber was proudly displayed at Forbes Air Force Base during an Armed Forces Day celebration in May 1958. The B-52, introduced in 1955, was the air force workhorse for 40 years. The aircraft sported eight turbo jet engines, giving it speed, range, and payload capacity. By 1963, the U.S. Air Force had 650 long-range bombers in operation. (Courtesy Kansas State Historical Society.)

A Boeing KC-97 Stratotanker links with a RB-47 in a refueling exercise over Forbes Air Force Base in this 1957 photograph. Manufactured by Boeing, the KC-97 Stratotanker became the world's first production aerial tanker in 1950. The piston-engine KC-97 used aviation gasoline but carried jet fuel for the RB-47s. In 1956, the air force began replacing the KC-97s with the faster jet-powered KC-135 Stratotanker. (Courtesy Kansas State Historical Society.)

Above, workers pour concrete for what was the world's longest runway, measuring 12,800 feet in length. It was completed in September 1955 at a cost of $5 million. When the air force's 21st Division moved to Forbes in 1951, it marked a time of growth for both the air base and Topeka. The base, itself, was rebuilt at a cost of $15 million to accommodate 8,500 members of the Strategic Air Command. (Courtesy Kansas State Historical Society.)

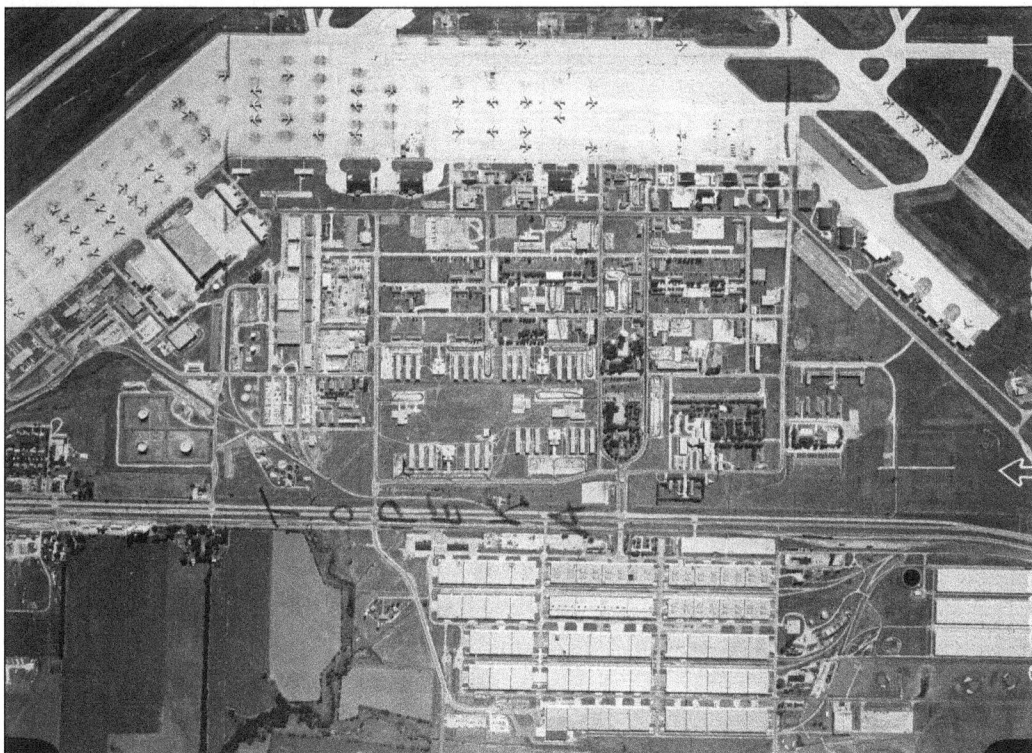

This aerial photograph of Forbes Air Force Base is dated July 23, 1963. Aircraft can be seen parked on the flight line. Topeka Boulevard can be seen running horizontally just below the center of the image, marked in pen. At this time, Forbes was a Strategic Air Command base and, arguably, the most powerful air force base in the world. (Courtesy Kansas State Historical Society.)

Above, a member of the 313th Tactical Airlift Wing loads a C-130 Hercules with humanitarian aid supplies bound for Amman, Jordan. Fighting between Palestinian guerrillas and the army of King Hussein had resulted in severe shortages of food and medical supplies. The 38th and the 47th Tactical Airlift Squadrons from Forbes joined in the airlift in October 1970, sporting Red Cross logos and paperwork. (Courtesy Combat Air Museum.)

This Atlas E missile launcher, located at Keene, Kansas, was the first operational site among the nine intercontinental ballistic missile bases of the 548th Strategic Missile Squadron at Forbes Air Force Base. By October 1961, all nine sites were armed. The Atlas E lay horizontally in a coffin silo and was hoisted upright for firing. The 548th Strategic Missile Squadron was activated on July 1, 1960, and deactivated on March 25, 1965. (Courtesy Ed Peden.)

Six

A DAY IN THE HISTORY OF TOPEKA

There are certain days that are marked in history, noteworthy for events that transpired at that time or events that cumulated on that day. There are a number of days that are so noted in the history of Topeka, and this chapter will examine five such days, recorded in history and with photographs.

On May 30, 1903, the Kansas River crested at 38.5 feet in Topeka in the worst flood that the city had experienced up to that time. The floodwaters had been growing since a series of storms and heavy rains had begun 10 days earlier. Flooding had been reported in Salina, Abilene, and Manhattan, but no one in Topeka imagined how bad the flood would be. When the river crested on Saturday night, much of North Topeka was under 10 feet of floodwater. The bottoms area along the south side of the river was flooded badly, as well. Three bridges were dislodged, making escape from North Topeka impossible except by boat. Many publications of the day described daring rescues by boat. Some of the rescue boats capsized, and those attempting to rescue stranded residents died in unsuccessful attempts.

Various sources report the loss of life in Topeka in far varying numbers. Some published accounts put the number of people to drown at 29. The U.S. Weather Service lists the loss of life in Topeka for the 1903 flood at 38 deaths. Katheryne Graves published a short book, *The Kaw Valley Deluge*, shortly after the flood in 1903. She claims that as many as 100 people lost their lives in Topeka from the flood and accompanying fires. In her book she reports that fires starting when lime stored at J. Thomas Lumber became wet, and that pieces of burning lumber then floated to other flooded structures, setting them afire.

The *New York Times* ran an article bearing a May 30, 1903, dateline reporting on the flooding and fires in Topeka. The article states, "North Topeka, isolated from the rest of the city by the flood is an island, on which fire and water are uniting to complete the destruction of the place. . . . Four hundred houses have burned, and as near as can be learned, about 150 persons are dead." The article goes on to detail the horrors of the flooded city.

Regardless of the report one chooses to believe, there has never been a loss of life in Topeka from any disaster that exceeded the casualties from the 1903 flood. More than 4,000 people lost their homes and all of their possessions.

On March 15, 1935, a powerful dust storm arose in the Texas and Oklahoma panhandles, sweeping across western Kansas and picking up more dirt, creating the first in a long series of dust storms. This day, dubbed "Black Friday," would mark the beginning of a month of dust storms that swept across the Midwest. The despair that Americans were feeling in the throes of the Great Depression was punctuated by the 1935 storms. A month later, on April 14, 1935, the fiercest dust storm of all would sweep across the county on what would be known as "Black Sunday."

The dust from the storms of 1935 would be followed by the record heat and drought of 1936. Many New Deal projects had provided enough work for Americans to survive, but times were tough. The number of people who have recollections of the Great Depression dwindles every day; however, good photographic records clearly depict the times.

On Friday, July 13, 1951, the Kansas River crested in Topeka at an all time high of 41.3 feet, according to the National Weather Service, making the 1951 flood the worst in Topeka history. The river remained above flood stage for 10 consecutive days, setting another record. Breaks in dikes along the Kansas River forced the evacuation of 24,000 people from North Topeka, Oakland, and other areas proximate to the river. Over 7,000 buildings in Topeka were damaged or destroyed. More than 700 people were rescued from roofs of homes in flooded areas. On that one unlucky Friday, four bridges spanning the Kansas River were lost, including the Brickyard Bridge; the Sardou Bridge; the Atchison, Topeka, and Santa Fe Railroad bridge; and the Rock Island Railroad bridge.

Amazingly, there are no reports of deaths by drowning from the 1951 flood in Topeka. Much of this can be attributed to excellent evacuation operations undertaken by the National Guard and city and county emergency services workers. The 1951 flood is well recalled by many in Topeka today, and there are expansive photograph collections made of the flood damage.

On May 17, 1954, the U.S. Supreme Court handed down a ruling in the case of Brown v. Board of Education, Topeka, outlawing racial segregation in public schools. In a unanimous decision, the court found that "separate educational facilities are inherently unequal." Although the case bore the name of Oliver Brown, there were actually five cases that had been consolidated and decided under the name Brown v. Board of Education, Topeka. The Brown family lived near Sumner Elementary School in Topeka; however, because they were African American, their daughter was forced to attend school at the all-black Monroe Elementary. The decision would be a major landmark in the civil rights movement, and it would change the face of public education in America.

On Wednesday, June 8, 1966, a massive tornado, measuring F5 in intensity, touched down in southwest Topeka near Burnett's Mound, traveling 22 miles across Topeka before lifting into the clouds as it passed out of the city. In its wake, the twister left 16 people dead and $100 million in property damage. It was estimated that 550 people were injured by the tornado, with 85 being admitted to local hospitals. The tornado destroyed 800 homes, while damaging 1,200 more in the city.

Everyone who was in Topeka on June 8, 1966, has vivid recollections of the sights and sounds of the storm. There has never been a single event in the history of the city that generated so many published photographs than this tornado and its aftermath. At least six special publications appeared at the time featuring tornado photographs and stories. Postcards featuring more than 100 views of the tornado and its destruction were sold. It was the most heavily photographed disaster in the history of Topeka.

This publication includes the most notable photographs taken of the tornado and its damage, including never-before-published views taken by the Topeka Police Department crime scene investigator Don Mogge. The images speak volumes about the storm.

While history is marked in days and recorded with words, it is most accurately portrayed in the photographs of the time.

This view of North Kansas Avenue during the 1903 flood shows four boats in the flooded avenue looking for stranded residents and business owners. The river crested at 38.5 feet on May 30, placing all of North Topeka and the bottoms south of the river under water. Three bridges over the Kansas River were dislodged, and more than 4,000 people, mostly from North Topeka, were left homeless. (Courtesy Kansas State Historical Society.)

This 1903 photograph shows the north side of the Melan Bridge on North Kansas Avenue. The floodwaters had washed away the approach to the bridge, and a wooden-plank gangway was constructed for people to get onto the bridge to escape the flooded North Topeka. The approaches on both ends of the bridge had to be replaced, but the Melan Bridge survived another 62 years. (Courtesy Kansas State Historical Society.)

There was simply no place to go for the 4,000 people left homeless by the 1903 flood in North Topeka. A tent city was established to provide a place for the homeless until new housing could be found. In addition to the flooding, lumberyards caught fire when water reacted to carbide, causing burning lumber to float into other structures, setting them afire. It was the largest disaster in Topeka's history. (Courtesy Greg Hoots.)

This interior view of the Topeka Provident Association, located at 335 Jackson Street, was taken soon after its founding in 1904. The organization was created in response to the great need created by the devastating 1903 flood. Above, African American girls are given cooking classes at the Topeka Provident Association. The organization provided other social services and, in 1951, changed its name to Family Service of Topeka. (Courtesy Kansas State Historical Society.)

New York governor Franklin D. Roosevelt addresses a crowd of 10,000 people from the steps of the Kansas statehouse in this September 14, 1932, photograph. It was a certain sign of the hard times that such a large crowd gathered to listen to the Democrat candidate who was running against a Republican ticket that included Topeka native vice president Charles Curtis. Some of the crowd undoubtedly included Kansas Free Fair goers; after speaking, Roosevelt's motorcade paraded to the fairgrounds to watch an automobile race on opening day of the fair. This stop in Topeka was Roosevelt's first campaign stop west of the Mississippi River. Interestingly, in those days, the presidential campaign did not begin until Labor Day. Roosevelt carried Kansas and the nation in a landslide election. (Courtesy Greg Hoots.)

The year 1935 saw a series of dust storms that beset Oklahoma and western Kansas. A few such storms reached Topeka, including this March 20, 1935 storm that darkened the skies in midday. Above, a thick layer of duct can be seen on cars from this view atop the National Bank Building, looking at the intersection of Sixth Avenue and Jackson Street. (Courtesy Kansas State Historical Society.)

The construction of the Topeka Avenue bridge was a $1.5 million Works Progress Administration project to span the Kansas River at Highway 75. Completed in 1938, the bridge served Topeka traffic for 68 years until its closing in August 2006. A new bridge at Topeka Avenue opened on August 4, 2008. (Courtesy Kansas State Historical Society.)

In the summer of 1940, Topeka celebrated the opening of the Topeka Municipal Airport. The Works Progress Administration built three asphalt runways bordered with drainage tiles and constructed the hanger (seen above), complete with storage area and lounge. Quite a crowd had gathered for the grand opening of the airport in this Kent Lyle photograph. (Courtesy Kansas State Historical Society.)

This Harold B. Wolfe night photograph of the new lit tennis courts at Gage Park is dated 1939. This was one of the many improvements of Gage Park that was funded with New Deal public works money. Wolfe, Topeka's preeminent commercial photographer, took pictures of all of the public works projects upon their completion for various government agencies. (Courtesy Special Collections, TSCPL.)

Above, this view of Kansas Avenue looking north from First Avenue was taken during the 1951 flood. A truck has apparently become stranded, and an attempt is being made to load the cargo into a boat. Notice that the Chesterfield Hotel (see page 61) can be seen at the far left. There is another boat going north on Kansas Avenue and one parked at Kaw Valley Produce. Below, boats were used to rescue North Topeka residents trapped in their houses by the floodwaters of the Kansas River. (Both, courtesy Lloyd Zimmer.)

The cloverleaf at the intersection of Highways 75 and 24 is seen in the Harold Wolfe aerial view of the 1951 flood. At left center, the Jayhawk Junior Motel stands flooded to the roof eaves. Behind the motel, the Topeka Owls baseball park on Lyman Road can be seen underwater. Wolfe's brother-in-law and partner, Harold Worswick, piloted an airplane for the former to photograph the flood damage throughout the city. (Courtesy Greg Hoots.)

This Anderson Photo Company aerial view of Topeka, dated July 13, 1951, shows the swollen Kansas River as it crested on July 13, 1951. The view looks north, and one can see downtown and the dome of the capitol building at the upper right. The flood level exceeded the measuring devices' capacities at the time; however, the National Weather Service lists it as 41.8 feet, a modern record. (Courtesy Kansas State Historical Society.)

The Monroe School, located at 1515 Monroe Street, was a segregated black elementary school that came to the forefront in the issue of school segregation. This Harold B. Wolfe photograph of the school was taken shortly after construction of the building was completed in 1927. On May 17, 2004, the National Park Service opened a historic site center at the former school. (Courtesy Kansas State Historical Society.)

Photographer John Edward Schrock photographed Edna Vance's second-grade class in its classroom in the Monroe Elementary school in this March 3, 1949, view. The board of education argued that insofar Monroe was a newer school and equal in all respects to the white schools, no breech of law had occurred. The U.S. Supreme Court disagreed, ruling that "separate but equal" was inherently unequal. (Courtesy Kansas State Historical Society.)

Sumner Grade School, constructed in 1936 by the Public Works Administration, was an all-white segregated elementary school that came to the forefront in the Brown v. Board of Education lawsuit. Oliver Brown lived only a few blocks from Sumner and wanted his daughter, Linda, to attend school there. As they were African American, the board of education had assigned her to attend the all-black Monroe Elementary. (Courtesy Kansas State Historical Society.)

This Schrock photograph of Marilyn Rogge's sixth-grade class at Lincoln Elementary School is dated March 3, 1959, five years after the Brown v. Board of Education decision was rendered. Interestingly, only the Topeka elementary schools were segregated at the time of the lawsuit. Both African American and whites had always attended Topeka High School, although the athletic teams were segregated. (Courtesy Kansas State Historical Society.)

On June 8, 1966, this deadly tornado tore through Topeka, claiming 16 lives and leaving millions of dollars of damage in its path. Above, the funnel comes over Burnett's Mound at 7:15 p.m. and bears down on Topeka. Residents and photographer Perry Riddle had taken cover at the Countryside Methodist Church at 3221 Burlingame Road as the twister approached. Riddle dashed out of the church to take this photograph, barely making it back inside the building before the tornado hit. (Courtesy Kansas State Historical Society.)

Above, looking south from Twenty-ninth Street at Gage Boulevard, a shadowy figure of a man surveys the wasteland created by the tornado. Shown at right, a bewildered resident of the Huntington Apartments near the same intersection finds a Corvair parked in her second-story apartment. Both of these photographs were included in the *Topeka Capital-Journal*'s special photographic supplement to the paper, "The Day the Sky Fell." The fury of the storm was consistent along its 22-mile path across the city. Damage from the twister was more than $100 million. Adjusted for inflation to today's dollars, the damage would have exceeded $650 million. (Both, courtesy Kansas State Historical Society.)

Minutes after the storm passed, rescue efforts begin. Above, men carry an injured woman on a makeshift stretcher formed from a door. This photograph was taken at Gage Boulevard looking west between Twilight Drive and Thirtieth Street Terrace. There were 16 fatalities from the Topeka tornado, with more than 550 people injured. Hospitals reported 85 people admitted to emergency rooms with tornado-related injuries. (Courtesy Kansas State Historical Society.)

Tom Coleman stands amid the rubble of what was his home at 232 Lime Street in Oakland. As is often the case with tornados, it was amazing what the storm took and what was spared. This view shows that his house was taken by the twister, yet his kitchen stove was left behind. The weather service reported 800 homes destroyed in Topeka, another 810 suffered major damage, and 400 had minor damage. (Courtesy Kansas State Historical Society.)

Every building on the Washburn campus was damaged by the tornado. Eight buildings were completely destroyed, while 14 sustained extensive damage such as Stoffer Hall, seen in this *Capital-Journal* photograph. Washburn University set the damage to its campus alone at $10 million. Miraculously, no one was killed on the campus, although Bertha Whitney died from injuries sustained at her residence at 1631 Washburn Avenue, across Seventeenth Street from the school. (Courtesy Kansas State Historical Society.)

This *Capital-Journal* photograph shows how difficult it was to even recognize neighborhoods after the storm. Within minutes of the storm's passage from the city, residents attempted to recover belongings that had been scattered by the storm. Traffic was completely halted throughout parts of Topeka as the streets were filled with storm debris. Police and emergency vehicles were plagued with flat tires from roofing nails torn from many destroyed houses. (Courtesy Kansas State Historical Society.)

Moments after the tornado struck the city, Topeka Police Department crime scene investigator Don Mogge was given the assignment to photograph the storm's path of destruction through town. Armed with a Graflex press camera and riding on a motor scooter, Mogge took 400 photographs of the storm damage, beginning at Burnett's Mound. These final eight photographs of the storm damage are never-before-published views captured by Mogge after the storm. Above, this view was taken looking south at Twenty-ninth Street and Gage Boulevard and shows the enormity of the damage. Below, after the storm, residents wandered the street in shock and disbelief. (Both, courtesy Lloyd Zimmer.)

Above, Central Park Elementary School, located at Fourteenth and Clay Streets, was destroyed by the tornado as it ripped through central Topeka. Below, at Washburn University, Rice Hall (center) and MacVicar Chapel (right) were completely destroyed by the tornado. Notice the cars upside down in the foreground and a helicopter flying overhead, assessing the damage. The tornado left a path of destruction 22 miles long, with a swath in the center of the city measuring 8 miles long and four blocks wide that suffered devastating losses. (Both, courtesy Lloyd Zimmer.)

In this view, taken near Twenty-ninth Street and Gage Boulevard, part of a building has been detached by the storm and deposited on a row of cars. Looking at this image with the photographer, Don Mogge, he pointed out the sign that had been placed in the rubble, just to the left of the cars, where a barbershop had once stood, reading, "MOVED TO RAMADA, BARBER SHOP BOB HELP." (Courtesy Lloyd Zimmer.)

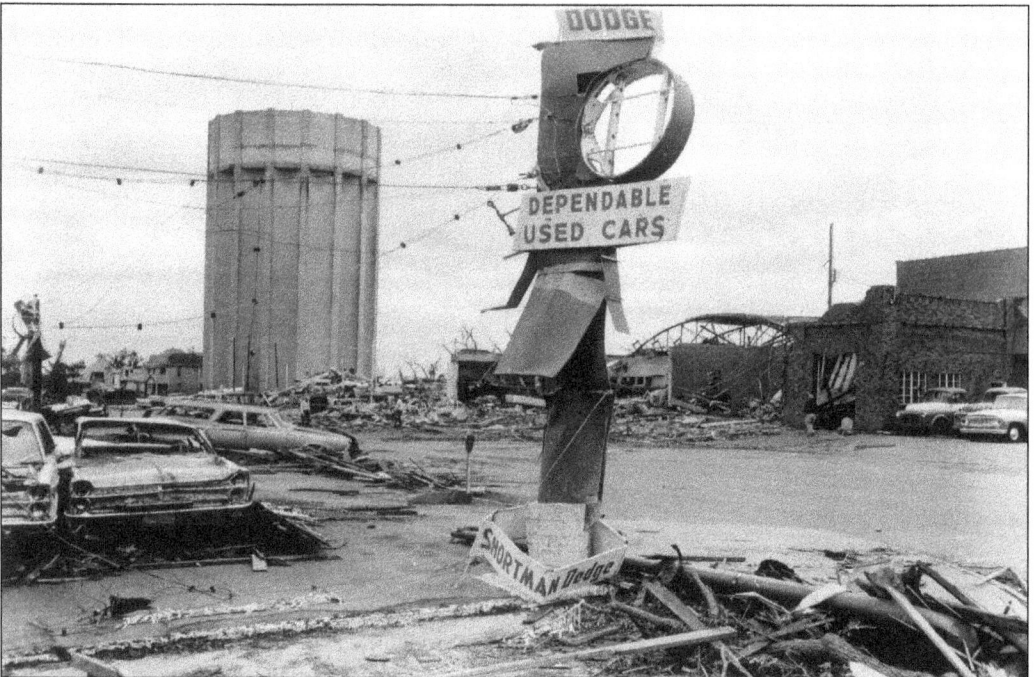

The Shortman Dodge car dealership, located at the southwest corner of Tenth Avenue and Quincy Street, was severely damaged by the winds; virtually every car at the dealership was badly damaged. This was a particularly hard hit area of the downtown. Nearby, the city transit bus garage was demolished, and 42 of the city's 50 busses were completely destroyed, an uninsured loss for the city of $250,000. (Courtesy Lloyd Zimmer.)

As the tornado completed its path across Topeka, it struck Billard Airport, badly damaging private aircraft. The U.S. Weather Service had its offices and reporting station at this airport. The top wind speed from the F5 tornado measured at the airport was 72 miles per hour. Weather service officials explained that the measuring instrument had been destroyed by the wind and that was simply its final reading. (Courtesy Lloyd Zimmer.)

Police investigator Don Mogge told this author that as he rode down Kansas Avenue on his motor scooter, he noticed the sign on the side of the National Reserve Life building, located at Tenth and Kansas Avenues, and stopped to take this photograph. The words were, "a refuge in the time of storm." Every window was blown out of the building, and much of the building's facing was damaged. (Courtesy Lloyd Zimmer.)

Visit us at
arcadiapublishing.com

www.ingramcontent.com/pod-product-compliance
Lightning Source LLC
Chambersburg PA
CBHW050703150426
42813CB00055B/2442